The French Revolution: The History and Legacy of the V Social Revolution

By Charles River Editors

Jean-Pierre Houël's "The Storming of the Bastille"

About Charles River Editors

Charles River Editors provides superior editing and original writing services across the digital publishing industry, with the expertise to create digital content for publishers across a vast range of subject matter. In addition to providing original digital content for third party publishers, we also republish civilization's greatest literary works, bringing them to new generations of readers via ebooks.

Sign up here to receive updates about free books as we publish them, and visit Our Kindle Author Page to browse today's free promotions and our most recently published Kindle titles.

Introduction

A depiction of the opening of the Estates-General on May 5, 1789

As one of the seminal social revolutions in human history, the French Revolution holds a unique legacy, especially in the West. The early years of the Revolution were fueled by Enlightenment ideals, seeking the social overthrow of the caste system that gave the royalty and aristocracy decisive advantages over the lower classes. But history remembers the French Revolution in a starkly different way, as the same leaders who sought a more democratic system while out of power devolved into establishing an incredibly repressive tyranny of their own once they acquired it.

The French Revolution was a turbulent period that lasted several years, and one of the most famous events of the entire revolution came near the beginning with the Tennis Court Oath. By July of 1788, King Louis XVI agreed to call the Estates-General, a large, traditional legislative body, for the first time since 1614. The country's finances, already quite tenuous, reached a crisis stage in August 1788 as France faced bankruptcy.

In March 1789, the electoral method was set. While the nobility and clergy would hold direct elections, the much larger Third Estate would elect representatives from each district who would then attend larger assemblies to elect their official representatives to the Third Estate of the Estates-General.

Finally, in the spring of 1789, Louis XVI summoned the Estates-General. They were to convene at Versailles on April 27, but did not do so until May 5. Late elections continued into the summer as conditions around the country delayed many elections. At the same time, bread prices reached an all-time high, leading to riots throughout the country, particularly in Paris. During the formal ritual that welcomed the Estates-General on May 4, 1789, in a precursor of things to come in the following months, the Third Estate refused to kneel before the king. The deputies of the Third Estate came before the king, walking two at a time, and bowed before Louis XVI and Marie Antoinette. Not surprisingly, those witnessing the parade of the Estates-General had hoped for reform but came to expect that the Estates-General would serve as a tool of the administration.

While the First and Second Estate argued over voting issues and methods, the Third Estate began to organize itself to a new degree. On June 7, a 30-year-old named Maximilien Robespierre made an impassioned speech criticizing the wealth of the clergy, which drew the attention of the entirety of the Third Estate. With certain members' encouragement, the Third Estate took the first steps toward declaring itself the National Assembly on June 10. Jean-Sylvain Bailly was chosen as President of the Third Estate, and by June 10, 1789, the Third Estate sent word to the other two estates, requesting that they join together and agree to common verification or vote by head. They received no response and opted to proceed without the consent or participation of the First and Second Estates. Thus, the Third Estate declared itself the only legitimate representative body, calling itself the "Commons". The public received the news with great support, and in the coming days, a few members of the clergy presented themselves. The "Commons" became the National Assembly on June 17, 1789, and two days later, the clergy officially joined the National Assembly.

As the Third Estate branded itself the National Assembly, Louis was more concerned with the death of the nine-year-old Dauphin. He and Marie Antoinette now had only two surviving children, Marie-Therese and Louis Charles, and the death of his eldest son had thrown Louis XVI into a period of depression and inaction. He was somewhat aware of the occurrences around them, but he did not perceive their importance.

While the king was largely unconcerned, the queen was more aware of the happenings around them. She, along with the Comte d'Artois, encouraged the war minister's efforts to reinforce army garrisons near Paris, whereas Finance Minister Jacques Necker supported conciliation and accommodation with the National Assembly. Necker suggested the king call a Royal Session to take place on June 22, both to reassert royal authority and offer a number of concessions, but the plans for the Royal Session proceeded without notification, and on June 20 the National Assembly found their doors locked and under guard.

Unaware of why the National Assembly was closed off, and faced with the loss of their usual meeting place, the National Assembly laid claim to an unused indoor tennis court at Versailles for their meetings, which continued throughout the weekend of June 20, 1789. The king's actions were viewed as an act of despotism, renewing the spirit of the Assembly. Together, all of the deputies of the National Assembly, took an oath, commonly referred to as the Tennis Court Oath, in which they vowed to remain in session until "the constitution of the Realm and public regeneration are established and assured."

On June 22, the Royal Session was postponed and the Assembly met again in the tennis court. They welcomed the clergy to the National Assembly, as decided on June 19. With some joy, they also greeted three noblemen from the Estates-General who had chosen to join the National Assembly. The stage was set for a confrontation between the king and the National Assembly.

Throughout the day on July 13, 1789, rumors of an impending attack by the French army spread through the city of Paris. A large mob formed, first taking some 28,000 rifles from the Invalides, the veterans' hospital in the city, and in search of powder for the rifles, the mob stormed the Bastille, an old and largely unused prison in the city. While the Bastille, with its imposing turrets and fort-like construction, was a symbol of oppression, their intent was less political and more practical; they needed ammunition, and the prison was under relatively light guard with only a few prisoners.

The guards first attempted to negotiate with the group, hoping to buy time for extra troops to arrive, but finally the guards fired on the mob when negotiations failed. Hundreds in the mob were killed, and when additional troops arrived, rather than defending the Bastille, they joined with the mob, providing canons and soldiering skills to ensure the success of the people over the Bastille guards. Late in the afternoon, the Bastille guards surrendered and were killed by the mob, while future revolutionaries like Robespierre supported the actions of the mob as a reflection of the will of the people, even when they killed the governor of the Bastille.

News of the incident at the Bastille reached the royal palace of Versailles the same day, but King Louis XVI did not respond or act, even when the Assembly requested he pull back troops from the city. Indeed, the royal response was mixed, with Queen Marie Antoinette favoring military action to put down the rebellion at once while Louis XVI continued to hope for some sort of peaceful solution. Louis eventually agreed to pull the troops back on the afternoon of July 15, and after some of his troops had joined the mob at the Bastille, Louis XVI now understood that he could not trust or rely upon the army. When he asked if it was a revolt, he was famously told that it was a revolution, and as news of the violence spread throughout the country, revolutionary groups took control of many city governments. Grain shortages led to outright rebellion in some areas as hungry people broke into granaries and landlords' estates, and pillage, destruction and arson impacted towns, cities and small rural communities throughout France. With that, the stage was set for the French Revolution to take its course.

The early years of the French Revolution were fueled by Enlightenment ideals, seeking the social overthrow of the caste system that gave the royalty and aristocracy decisive advantages over the lower classes. But history remembers the French Revolution in a starkly different way, as the same leaders who sought a more democratic system while out of power devolved into establishing an incredibly repressive tyranny of their own once they acquired it.

The height of Republican France's tyranny came during a 10 month period forever known as the Reign of Terror, the most notorious and arguably most memorable part of the French Revolution. One of the first victims of the Reign of Terror was its most famous: former French Queen Marie Antoinette. But Antoinette was followed by thousands more, including everyone from aristocrats to clergy to prostitutes and even instrumental revolutionaries like Danton, Desmoulins, and, most notably, Robespierre. It was Robespierre whose position on the Committee of Public Safety made him the Reign of Terror's instrumental figure until he himself became a victim of it in July 1794. Robespierre's date with the guillotine is often considered the official end of the Reign of Terror, but by then it is estimated that at least 16,000 people were guillotined in that time and possibly 25,000 more were summarily executed across the country.

Although Robespierre is almost singlehandedly associated with the Reign of Terror and is typically blamed for it, many factors influenced the actions and beliefs of Paris and the remainder of France during late 1793 and 1794. Robespierre and the Committee of Public Safety believed passionately in the Revolution and fought to eliminate any threat to the young French Republic. Robespierre envisioned a Republic of Virtue, with no room for anyone who did not abide by his rules and morality. Counterrevolutionaries certainly did threaten the Revolution, but most of those killed during the Reign of Terror were not counterrevolutionaries and posed no serious threat to the Revolution or Republic.

While the Terror came to an end with Robespierre's death in July 1794, the end result was not exactly peace. Economic conditions continued to worsen throughout the end of 1794. Food was not only expensive, but extremely scarce in some areas. On December 24, price controls were eliminated, recreating the free market. The winter of 1794 to 1795 was especially bad. While wheat and rice were purchased and subsidized to prevent starvation, fuel shortages worsened the situation. The government went into debt to provide bread rations, but those were becoming less accessible by the spring of 1795. By May of 1795, driven by hunger, the sans-culottes began to organize once again. Bread rations had been cut to as little as one-quarter pound each day. A brief and unsuccessful attempt to call for an insurrection to put the constitution of 1793 and additional bread rations into place followed.

The chaos would continue for several more years, and France's new direction would not truly be decided until a Corsican military officer by the name of Napoleon Bonaparte reached the apex of power in the country. By the end of 1799, France remained rife with political tensions - the recently constituted Directory was viewed as supine and ineffective by the people, and their situation was worsened by a combination of years of internal and external war which, coupled with an enemy naval blockade, had virtually bankrupted the country. France was ready for change.

Napoleon was offered a chance to be a part of that change when one of the Directors, Emmanuel Sieyes, included him in his scheme to stage a coup against the Directory and seize power. Never one to turn down a chance for advancement, Napoleon agreed, and on November 9th, as false rumors of a Jacobin uprising (started by the plotters themselves) spread through the city, he took charge of a detachment of troops and escorted key members of the Directory away from their seat in Paris, to the nearby residence of Chateau Saint-Cloud. When members of the Directory realized that something suspicious was afoot, they attempted to protest, at which point Napoleon ordered his men to advance on them with bayonets. With the majority of the legislators thus dispersed, Napoleon was able to coerce or convince the remainder to name himself, Sieyes and another of the plotters, Roger Ducos, temporary Consuls and effective rulers of France.

Emmanuel Sieyes had always imagined Napoleon would take a subordinate role in the governing of the country and be grateful for being involved in the plot, but Sieyes had severely underestimated who he was dealing with. Just a little over a month after the coup, Napoleon drafted a constitution, known as the Constitution of the Eighth Year of the Republic, which placed virtually all legislative and executive powers in the hands of the First Consul and relegated the remaining two to subordinate roles. Having already outfoxed foes on the battlefield, Napoleon displayed his skills in the political realm by now outwitting Sieyes badly; Napoleon managed to get himself elected First Consul, and thus by extension he had become the de facto monarch of France. With that, the Napoleonic Era would begin in earnest.

The *Ancien Régime* and the Third Estate

In the late 18th century, France was one of the most powerful nations in the world with a monarchy that could trace its lineage for many hundreds of years. However, the country was also virtually bankrupt and a large proportion of its population lived in conditions little different to the serfdom of the Middle Ages.

In France, as in most other contemporary European countries, the king ruled by "divine right". This meant that the monarch had absolute power and was not answerable to his subjects or to any other body or group. There was no formal elected government in the modern sense but the people of France were divided into three "estates." Each estate had access to power principally through its influence on the king.

The First Estate was the clergy. The Church had great power in France (as in most other contemporary European states) and its members were given a number of privileges. They were not, for example, required to pay taxes though many senior members of the church accumulated great personal wealth. The First Estate was relatively small, representing less than one half of one percent of the total population, but it enjoyed a high level of influence with the monarch and was able to use this to ensure that its own power and wealth were protected.

The Second Estate consisted of the hereditary nobility of France. This was a far larger group totaling around 400,000 people. The nobility was not only exempt from paying many taxes, it was permitted to levy its own taxes on subjects who lived on land it owned. As this group owned around 25% of all the land in France, this became an important source of wealth for the nobility. Only members of the First and Second Estates could be appointed as advisors to the king, foreign ambassadors, and senior leaders in the army and navy. Essentially, only members of these two estates had the right to be appointed to positions of honor and political power within the French state.

That left everyone else, around 98% of the total population, in the Third Estate. The majority of these people were laborers and peasants, largely uneducated and often living in conditions of extreme poverty and hardship. Despite this, the main burden of taxation fell upon members of this group. However, by the latter half of the 18th century, a new group was emerging within the Third Estate; the *bourgeoisie*.

These were often families of educated professional men, including lawyers, merchants and doctors. Many members of the *bourgeoisie* were wealthy, in some cases far more wealthy than impoverished noble families, but they were excluded from positions of power and influence within France. It was amongst this group that radical new ideas first found widespread support.

During the 18th century a number of philosophers and writers began to become interested in a new approach to the organization of the state. There were a number of different views but their ideas became known as the "*enlightenment.*" These ideas were very radical and posed a direct threat to those in positions of power by questioning things like the divine right of monarchs to rule the mass of people. Some, like Genevan philosopher Jean-Jacques Rousseau, went even further, questioning the whole basis of hereditary nobility and the notion of a population divided by class.

The American Revolution, which lasted from 1775-1783, focused even more attention on these ideas. The English colonists in the thirteen colonies on the east coast of the present-day United States objected to the fact that they were required to pay taxes to the English government but were given no representation within that government. "Taxation without representation is tyranny" became a rallying cry for colonists who sought independence but it also struck a chord with many other people who found themselves trapped within systems of government that gave them no voice and no influence.

When the colonists were victorious and declared the emergence of a new country, the United States of America, they did so with the adoption of a constitution based on social democracy, something that was revolutionary in every sense. Even the Declaration of Independence itself was couched in language that threatened the social order in virtually every other country, beginning with an iconic assertion: "We hold these truths to be self-evident, that all men are created equal, that they are endowed by their Creator with certain unalienable rights, that among these are life, liberty and the pursuit of happiness."

In countries like France, ruled by absolute monarchs and a small coterie of aristocrats, this was dangerous talk that threatened the very fabric upon with society was based. The French nation was based upon that principle that all men were <u>not</u> created equal and that some, by nothing more than accident of birth, had rights to power and influence while the majority did not. To Kings and their supporters, the enlightenment threatened everything they had and aspired to.

All of these things might have mattered less if France had been affluent, but it was not. Throughout the 18th century, France had fought a series of wars against Britain and other countries. These had been, almost without exception, disasters both in military and economic terms. Louis XV, King of France from 1715-1774, fought the Seven Years' War (1756-1763) against Britain. France led a coalition that included the Holy Roman Empire, Spain and Russia against a British coalition that included Prussia and Portugal. The war was immensely costly and led to the utter defeat of the French coalition. The king spent the rest of his reign trying to build up a navy powerful enough to challenge the British at sea, but he succeeded only in creating massive debt.

His grandson, Louis XVI, managed to avoid direct conflict with the British but provided huge levels of financial and material support for the rebellious colonists in America. In total, France spent around a million livres, a staggering sum, on support for the colonists, but France gained little from the colonists' victory other than increased interest in revolutionary ideas. By the time that war was over, France was virtually bankrupt and, because of the organization of the three estates, tax revenue could only be obtained from the Third Estate.

At the same time that the war in America was ending, another event would have a profound effect on the people of France. In June 1783, Laki volcano in Iceland began to erupt. The eruption would last for eight months, spewing tons of ash and gas into the atmosphere and causing a haze that darkened the sky as far away as Syria. Due to this, the winter of 1783/1784 was particularly harsh and there were droughts throughout Europe in the summers of 1784 and 1785. For almost the ten years following the eruption, summers in Europe were less productive and in France, the most populous country in Europe, grain crops were particularly badly affected.

The shortage of grain quickly led to an increase in the price of bread, a matter of extreme concern to the poorest members of French society. Bread was one of the most important elements of diet for ordinary families. Even before the eruption of Laki and the poor summers that followed, peasants and laborers across France were spending up to half their wages on bread alone[1] and the supply of bread was so essential to maintaining order that bakers were considered to be public servants and bread production was controlled and monitored by the police. When bread prices rose sharply following the crop failures, hunger became a problem for many members of the Third Estate. But the taxes needed to pay off France's national debt could be raised only from this portion of the population. The scene was set for a confrontation between the monarchy, supported by the clergy and the nobles, and the disposed mass of French people.

The *ancien régime* ("old rule") in France, the social and political system with the king as absolute ruler, dated back to Medieval times when the kingdom of France was attempting to establish control over competing kingdoms within present-day France. This system had entered its absolutist phase during the reign of Louis XIV (1643 – 1715).

Under the rule of Louis XIV, also known as the "Sun King" (Roi Soleil), the feudal sovereignty of the nobility, previously a source of autonomous power within France, had been deliberately reduced. The king, fearing intrigue and possible opposition from the nobility, had built a great new Royal Palace at Versailles. He declared this to be his formal residence in 1682 and demanded that the most powerful nobles live in the palace. This allowed him to maintain direct control over the aristocracy who became both guests and hostages of the king.

From that time on, French kings became not only the regents by divine right but also heads of state, their administrators. This absolute control over the nobility made it impossible for it to manage its domains in any way except according to the will of the sovereign. The centralization achieved by Louis XIV would create a group under "the same laws, the same regulations and the same taxes"[2] consistent with a famous quote attributed to him: "I am the state"[3].

---

[1] Neely, S. *A Concise History of the French Revolution,* Rowman & Littlefield Publishers, London, 2007.
[2] Ibid., 7.

The creation of "intendants", the king's administrative agents, throughout France was a response to the centralization of the country and to the tax burden on all French inhabitants[4]. This administrative system differed from the feudal order because it owed its origin to the necessity of administrating a much larger society.

But tribute was not the only way in which this absolutist monarchy supported itself. It also raised money by selling titles to the aristocracy. By then, "the monarchic state had generally renegotiated the form of ancient privileges", and found financing by "loans through one or more of the bodies in the realm: the order of clergy, the city government of Paris or the Company of the king's Secretaries"[5]. The permanence of these privileges was linked to the debt that the state contracted with the privileged classes, which, in this way, "played the role of a vast bank for the government"[6].

At the same time, those who became members of the upper state at Versailles were forced to abandon any commercial initiatives, limited by the customs of the position they bought and the economic opportunities they brought.

Some of these opportunities were, for example, occupying positions in institutions of justice by hereditary right, something that "dated only from the 17th century"[7]. That is to say, members of noble families owned public offices and were able to make money through these. In this sense, the *ancien régime* had given birth to an economic regime long before the revolution took place.

Because they were prohibited from commerce, gradually, many noble families gradually became relatively poor. Being forced to live in the Royal Palace limited their ability to run their vast estates and many became entirely dependent on the generosity (or otherwise) of the king. The king also had the sole right to allow members of the nobility to enter positions of power and this was also used as a means to ensure their compliance with the king's wishes. At the same time, some members of the growing bourgeoisie were becoming wealthy. The result was a society in which "many rich people are not noble and many noble are not rich"[8].

Members of the bourgeoisie could not become nobles, no matter how wealthy they were, so they could never attain public offices of real power. They could join the clergy, but only in its lower levels – senior positions within the clergy were appointed by the king and were filled exclusively by nobles. This caused great resentment between the *bourgeoisie* and the king and his noble followers.

---

[3] "l'État, c'est moi" in French.
[4] Shennan, *Louis XIV*, 18.
[5] Furet, *The French Revolution, 1770-1814*, 7.
[6] Ibid., 8.
[7] Ibid.
[8] Escohotado, *Los enemigos del comercio I*, 483.

Modernity gave some members of the *bourgeoisie* (merchants, for example) access to great wealth due to industrial development and economic liberalism. In their view, however, their growing role in society was not consistent with the power that the upper classes had over them. They did not enjoy the privileges given to nobles but knew well that they financed them. Their taxes became an important contribution to the wealth of the crown. Their resentment at this situation would lead directly to demands by the Third Estate for reform.

However, the nobles were not happy either. The king's insistence that they reside at Versailles limited their opportunities to make money from their estates. The generosity of the king was severely limited by the fact that successive wars meant that the state was not just in debt, it was edging towards bankruptcy. The nobles became resentful as they saw members of the bourgeoisie becoming wealthy and they blamed the king for many of their troubles.

Marriages between businessmen and nobles became more common, with the former hoping to improve their social status and the latter seeking to increase their wealth. However, these marriages were relatively rare, and, in most instances, there was an unbridgeable social gulf between the bourgeoisie and the nobles. This led to resentment between these two social groups who were united only by their resentment at the power and prestige of the king.

By the latter third of the 18th century, the *ancien régime* looked from the outside as powerful and secure as it had ever been. The truth was very different. There was constant friction between the monarchy and both nobles and the bourgeoisie. New ideas such as the enlightenment and events such as the American War of Independence began to cause people to doubt not just the authority of the king but the question of whether he really was appointed by God.

The notion of separating societies into estates had existed since the medieval period. The king ruled according to God's will, the nobility supported the king and no-one else except the clergy were considered significant. Commercial activity was badly thought of, and mostly banned up until the Late Middle Ages, but despite this the *bourgeoisie* became a key component in the modernization of Europe as an industrial and commercial continent. And yet, the political power of this class was minimal as it remained part of the Third Estate.

In feudal times, merchants were subjects who operated on the margins of legality, frowned upon by the nobility and condemned by the clergy. However, they were generally accepted as long as their commercial work was needed. However, not all members of the Third Estate in France were members of the *bourgeoisie*. Far more were farmers, laborers and peasants who were burdened, in addition to the weight of taxes, with obligations to the nobility inherited from the *ancien régime*. The so-called "*corvée*" established that they, being still servants, owed their workforce and goods to the will of their lords who could dispose of them as they saw fit[9].

---

[9] Ibid., 483.

In this country of simmering discontent, the new and radical ideas of some philosophers found fertile ground, especially with the educated intellectuals of the enlightened *bourgeois*. These people began to gather in clubs, cafes, salons with Paris their as their epicenter. But in these places not only would a new way of thinking form, but also an antipathy to the old political and social institutions, as well as a movement against the clergy with which this new philosophy did not find any kinship at all. In fact, the followers of the enlightenment in France generally became profoundly anti-Catholic, resenting a church that was completely linked to the monarchy (Louis XVI was a fervent Catholic) and personally to noble titles.

The sale of titles of nobility was condemned to the same degree. This monetization of the nobility meant that the king was seen as nothing but another capitalist, and therefore not fit to be involved in the election of public offices. On this point members of the Third Estate were agreed; appointment to public office was something that, for the good of France, should be based on merit, not used by the king as a means of raising revenue.

At the same time, the French Enlightenment saw how in North America, and under French auspices, a non-monarchical government could appear. It was also pointed out that in England, France's traditional enemy, there was a bicameral monarchical government, a model of government that was be regarded with enthusiasm by both those who sought change and supporters of the king.

Regarding these subversive ideas, the monarchy could do little. The king had no control over public opinion, and although press freedom was not guaranteed, the proliferation of publications overpowered any serious attempts at censorship.

The political philosophical background of the coming revolution had its roots in the ideas of the Enlightenment. Perhaps the person who best synthesized how the Enlightenment was lived and thought of at the time was the Prussian philosopher Immanuel Kant, who defined it as the advent of humanity to its adulthood, or in his own words, "the exit of human beings from their self-incurred immaturity"[10]. The idea of leaving childhood implies, on the one hand, the chance for humanity to interpret and evaluate what has it done up to this point, and on the other, to put itself beyond it, having become responsible for its own will from then on.

The scientific advances of modernity did not stop at the natural sciences, as philosophers also turned to the realm of political discourse. Starting from Descartes, reason became the metaphysical center of human order, replacing divinity. As such, in political philosophy reason was meant to be synonymous with law and right. Politics, human order in society, was to be thought of only through the filter of reason and this was regarded as no less universal than the laws of nature. Kant himself understood natural rights as something to be adopted throughout the world and by every society within it[11]. The French revolution can be understood, first of all, as

---

[10] Fleischacker, *What Is Enlightenment?*, 13.

the advent of rights, understood as the product of nature, but to be guaranteed by man's work, as opposed to the divine right understood as a product of divinity. Divine sovereignty over earthly matters would pass into the hands of man through reason and law.

To the dispossessed members of the Third Estate, and particularly to the educated *bourgeois*, these ideas combined with the success of the revolution in America seemed to suggest that a better, more equitable society was possible.

The idea of natural rights comes from the belief that mankind had a primary state (a "natural" state) which can give an insight into how society should work on a perfect level. For some, it seemed clear that humanity should try to return to this perfect state, while for others it was clear that it should learn from it, but that a return was plainly impossible. One way or the other, "natural right was the dominant language of political reform for a wide range of eighteenth-century writers"[12].

In this way, this golden age myth, "in which individuals were social and equal, no one ruled over anyone else, and virtue came naturally"[13], can be read in Montesquieu, Voltaire and Rousseau's works, the most influential French philosophers before the revolution. Still common in Western culture, this idea was at that time "a set-piece in royalist propaganda from the Renaissance onward"[14], and made it easy to win followers for one side or the other. For this task, writers were central figures of the new political ideas of the century, frequently setting themselves against absolutism: "The fusion of natural right and republicanism into a single new political language did not originate in works of political theory but of literature (understood widely as belles lettres). The most radical transformation that these imaginative (and often imaginary) retellings introduced was the elimination of contractualism—that is, the doctrine that humans pass from a state of nature into civil society as the result of an implicit or explicit contract. Instead, works such as Fénelon's Télémaque and Montesquieu's Lettres persanes depicted societies (those of the Boeticans and the good Troglodytes, respectively) that existed in a revised state of nature.[15]"

Diving into its rhetoric, the natural state of mankind was seen as idyllic insofar as it did not require the writing of laws. These, it was claimed, were only necessary as humanity abandoned its natural state and became prone to impinge on each other's rights: "The only laws that they recognized were the unchanging laws of nature, which lie within us; by extension, there was no need to write them down or to inscribe them in a constitution. Natural right alone, however, was incapable of preserving these virtuous societies over time; even if men were naturally good, they

---

[11] Kant, *Filosofía de la historia*, 22.

[12] Edelstein, *The Terror of Natural Right: Republicanism, the Cult of Nature, and the French Revolution*, 8.

[13] Ibid., 11.

[14] Ibid., 13.

[15] Ibid., 11.

could be corrupted.[16]"

In a constitution, the natural rights work as axioms of the liberties and rights of citizens, as in a previous stage of their humanity. Compared to divine right, where the laws and mandates are not written on paper, republicanism lies on the other side of the political spectrum since "from Livy to Machiavelli and from Milton to Madison [...] republicanism was always centered around a constitution"[17]. Although the monarchy followed a list of tacit rules and customs, the new order demanded the force of the written word, for this canceled arbitrary judgment and provided equality for all those under its auspices.

The Constitution of the nascent United States was often used of an exemplar of the kind of written constitution in which the rights of all citizens were enshrined at the most basic level. For the members of the Third Estate, this was something to aspire to. To the monarchy and the nobility, it was something to be profoundly feared.

Lit de Justice

King Louis XVI of France has been blamed by many for the French Revolution, and for over 200 years it has been claimed by some historians that he might have been able to mitigate its effects or perhaps even avoid it altogether had he acted differently. Of course, modern historians have the benefit of hindsight, but the personality and views of the king were certainly important during events that would finally lead to revolution.

The son of the Dauphin Louis, who was the older son of Louis XV, Louis XVI took up the throne in 1784 at the age of 29. The fussy, introverted Louis XVI has been generally depicted by scholars as weak, hesitant and incapable, especially compared with his two predecessors. As historian Francois Furet put it, "It is easy to see how historians have been able to turn this average man into a hero, an incompetent, a martyr or a culprit: this honourable king, with his simple nature, ill adapted for the role he had to assume and the history which awaited him, can equally well inspire emotion at the unfairness of fate or an indictment against his lack of foresight as a sovereign. Where personal qualities were concerned, Louis XVI was not the ideal monarch to personify the twilight of royalty in the history of France; he was too serious, too faithful to his duties, too thrifty, too chaste and, in his final hour, too courageous. But through his visceral attachment to tradition, the adolescent who had spent his youth clinging to his aunts' apron-strings and in the shadow of the parti dévot, would be the man of a monarchy which was no longer suited to him or the era.[18]"

The truth is that Louis XVI was not so much incompetent as bound to two institutions of the

---

[16] Ibid.

[17] Ibid., 2.

[18] Furet, *The French Revolution, 1770-1814*, 30.

past: ancient royal customs and the selling of privileges held by the French state from the times of Louis XIV. Believing blindly in the former ruined his multiple attempts to cancel the latter. In having to carry the monarchy forward, Louis XVI should have reformed it first, but by the time he assumed the crown, it may already have been too late.

At the beginning of his reign, Louis XVI was initially popular. He was favored for his youth and goodwill, and he replaced a king (his grandfather) who had become so unpopular that his funeral had to take place at night for fear of causing popular unrest. Louis XVI's public image, however, was damaged by his spouse, Marie-Antoinette, and by his severely reactionary court. It was the latter that caused problems for him by greatly favoring the departure of his first designated minister of finances and opposing his revolutionary economic measures.

King Louis XVI by Antoine-François Callet

Marie Antoinette at age 13 by Martin van Meytens

On the other hand, his wife harmed his image as far as public opinion was concerned, as well as within the royal court. For the French people, the fact she was Austrian was held against her. The marriage had been arranged in the hope of reducing the hostility between the two nations, and yet it never overcame the fact that she was seen by many as an internal agent of foreigners. She was perceived more as an enemy than as an ally of the French cause.

Gossip and rumor had been prevalent in France since the first half of the 18th century, when the charge of witchcraft was made against Father Girard, leading to a revolt in which a crowd almost burned the house of the Jesuits in Paris[19]. In the case of Marie-Antoinette, her loss of prestige came from false rumors and grievances, added to the squandering of money in Versailles which she sponsored. Her position as the queen did not protect her against the press, which had a great facility for delivering sensationalist stories with virtually no truth to them. Popular opinion about her was so negative that, in the context of economic crisis and food shortages, she was accused of telling the starving poor that they should eat cake when told of the hard times the French people were going through.

As for Versailles and her court, the queen's personality did not help there either. Marie-Antoinette arrived in France knowing very little about the political machinations of the court, and most members remained wary of her influence and of the letters she regularly exchanged with her family in Austria. In the same way, the fact that the marriage took years to consummate and the rumors of her multiple lovers was another weapon used to damage both her and her husband's images.

Both the common people and the nobility became even more hostile towards her when she was accused of a scam carried out against the Cardinal of Roha. Although she was not part of the plot, which involved the purchase of "a necklace worth nearly two million livres"[20] in her name, she was still identified as guilty in the eyes of the public. With this incident, the general image of the monarchy, the court, and even the nobility was negatively affected.

It also happened that the extraordinary expenses of the monarchy slipped through scrutiny as administrative expenses since there was no autonomy between one office and the other. Thus, close friends and sympathizers of the queen received pensions in the same way as any public official. Truth be told, these expenses were but a little part of those used to maintain the French state, but they affected the image of the monarchy a great deal.

The inability of Louis XVI to persuade the royal court to carry out his policies was the "abdication of the monarchy before the aristocracy"[21]. In this sense, the nobility, blinded completely by its intransigence, did nothing but facilitate the Revolution. The main aggravating factor was the economic crisis that France was going through. The country was in debt, and the burden of this debt, of providing for the whole society, fell wholly upon the Third Estate. But while other monarchies had resolved to give up their privileges in order to achieve economic stability by equal taxation, France's nobles did not respond to the social crisis in the same way.

What finally condemned the French monarchy to not being able to make the changes required to perpetuate itself and prevent the revolution (or at least the violence that took the monarch's head) was its inability to backtrack with what had in the first place financed the creation of the French state: the sale of titles. The relationship between the monarchy and the nobility was

[19] Michelet, *La bruja*, 319-340.
[20] Furet, *The French Revolution, 1770-1814*, 32.
[21] Ibid.

heavily compromised by this issue, and when the time came to face the Revolution, there was no strength or union that could restrain it.

Meanwhile, the other monarchies of advanced European countries, such as England and Austria, were more flexible and negotiated with the Third Estate (the "*commons*") in a way that the French monarchy could not. They both rescinded the tax exemption for nobility and clergy. France, on the other hand, was unable to do so since this would have been extraordinarily expensive to the main supporters of the king. The state also could not afford to cease selling titles to the nobility. Annually, these sales were worth the equivalent of an average of five million pounds[22], a significant portion of state income.

However, it should be noted that the French state of the late 18th century was not completely reactionary. The centralization policies that began with Louis XIV cemented what would soon become a state machine capable of making policies with a wide scope and degree of effectiveness. In this system, the intendants were "well and truly in command, outranking the traditional authorities and with a finger in every foot"[23]. Endowed with the first national-scale demographic statistics in French history, their functions were directed towards fulfilling the progression that this new state promised to bring with it, reaching positions hitherto monopolized by old institutions. In this way, as result of their actions France was, at that time, said to be "the least feudal country in Europe"[24].

This centralization translated into a reduction of the power of the nobility, many of whom did not even own land. Despite the value of inheritance, money gained ground as a decisive arbiter of power, even more so when considering how state privileges had become paid for. In this manner, the old nobility, to differentiate themselves from these new nobles, became more entrenched by requiring, in their circles, a lineage of at least four generations as a sign of the true aristocrat.

The main reform, however, was one which the monarchy was not able to enforce until it was too late and the French Revolution was already a reality. This involved a reduction in the sale of titles and an end to the total exemption of the clergy and the nobility from paying taxes. Under the king's direct mandate some reforms were carried through; state pensions were reduced, new taxes were applied and the payments of certain debts were postponed, which ultimately gave more time for the economy to level off.

But despite noble opposition, political power remained firmly in the hands of the Monarch. All they could do was to oppose him or agree with him, but they were able to do little by themselves. This situation was made worse by the actions of Louis XVI who responded to calls for change

---

[22] Escohotado, *Los enemigos del comercio I*, 484-485.
[23] Furet, *The French Revolution, 1770-1814*, 10.
[24] Ibid., 16.

and reform by switching unpredictably *"between despotism and capitulation"*[25].

Right around the time the American Revolution started, Louis XVI replaced Finance Minister Anne-Robert-Jacques Turgot with Jacques Necker, a Protestant from Geneva, which at the time was an independent republic. Necker was a skilled banker with a great deal of experience who, in 1775, published a treatise objecting to free trade in the grain industry. The royal ministers had to be Catholic, so Necker was made Director of the Royal Treasury and later Controller-General of Finance. Necker attempted to manage the French financial crisis by taking out loans, spreading the tax burden over a wider range of the population, and using higher interest rates, rather than raising taxes. He also planned to reduce spending and reorganize the financial administration of the government. He imposed no new taxes, but he financed French involvement in the American Revolution with loans.

Turgot

[25] Ibid., 13.

Necker

In 1778, Necker established provincial administrations consisting of one-quarter nobles, one-quarter clergy and one-half landowners. While only two provincial administrations were created during Necker's administration, these two administrations were quite successful and operated smoothly long after Necker's resignation.

In 1781, Necker published an accounting of royal finances. His accounting presented a relatively positive image of the state finances and one which was utterly untrue. The Comte Rendu au Roi brought public finance to the attention of the people for the first time and was intended to provide the people with information and a greater understanding of government. Necker represented the interest payments the crown made on its substantial debt as nothing more than typical expenses to create a much more favorable impression. He later published the Financial Summary for the king, which presented an even more positive picture of state income and debts.

When Necker demanded extra power in 1781, the king refused. Marie Antoinette strongly disliked and distrusted Necker and may have influenced Louis' decision. In protest, Necker resigned and spent the next several years writing a three-volume text about the administration of government finance.

On August 6, 1787, Louis XVI held a lit de justice, enabling him to register new laws and reforms without the approval of parlement. The king held the ceremony at Versailles, well away from the chaos and large groups that had gathered to call for the Estates-General in Paris, and at the lit de justice, Louis called for new taxes and announced a number of spending cuts.

The lit de justice itself was quite calm, but the response of parlement was not. The next day, parlement condemned the forced registration of new taxes, declaring it illegal, and over the next few days, the Parlement de Paris voted to condemn Calonne for mismanagement of public funds. By August 15, the king exiled the Parlement de Paris, which initially brought protests in Paris, but the situation calmed by early September after government forces cleared the streets, closed clubs and clamped down on bookshops. The crown retained control, but parlements throughout France began to register their objections to royal policy.

While financial and political problems troubled France, there were significant tensions growing in the Dutch Republic. Patriots from the Dutch Republic had clashed with a Prussian, the Hohenzollern Princess of Orange, and Prussian troops entered the Dutch Republic in mid-September with the support of Great Britain. Within weeks, the Prussians controlled all of the Dutch Republic. Long an ally of France, the Dutch Republic had good reason to expect French aid, but it was not forthcoming. The financial crisis in France had become so severe that the crown could no longer meet obligations to its political allies.

Brienne proposed a comprehensive five-year plan to restore French credit and improve the overall finances of the French government. His plan did not call for new taxes, but it did require that two extant taxes be extended. He also agreed to present a full accounting of the finances of the French government. In mid-September, Brienne negotiated the return of the Parlement de Paris following their usual autumn break, and the Parlement de Paris was expected to return to the city in November. The Parisian response was varied, but on the whole, there was little hope for Brienne's plan. Nevertheless, Brienne's own optimism continued, and he believed that the Estates-General might be called in 1792 to mark the successful completion of his five-year plan.

On November 19, 1787, the Parlement de Paris convened in a rare royal session with the king in attendance. The king opened the session with an announcement of civil rights for Protestants, which was of particular importance as refugees entered the country from the Dutch Republic. Parlement argued for more than eight hours, but in the end, the Parlement de Paris did not vote on the five-year plan or the loans that would be required to finance government during these years. At the end of the day's discussion, Louis XVI simply announced the registration of the loans without parliamentary approval and promised the Estates-General would be called no later than 1792.

The Duc d'Orleans, head of the junior branch of the royal family, immediately protested the legality of the king's actions. The king, words failing him, stated that he did not care and it was legal because he wished it to be legal. The king left Parlement, but the session was not dismissed. Discussion continued for nearly four more hours that night and Parlement denounced the registration of the loans. The following day, Orleans and several other leaders of the Parlement de Paris were immediately exiled by lettres de cachet from the king, and in response, Parlement declared lettres de cachet illegal in January 1788. Provincial parlements across France began to refuse to register laws in protest of the king's actions, and accusations of despotism began in earnest.

Louis Philippe Joseph d'Orléans, Duke of Orleans

The Parlement de Paris issued a declaration on the fundamental laws of the realm on May 3, 1788. These fundamental laws included the right of parlements to register new laws, the role of the Estates-General and the freedom of all French subjects from arbitrary arrest. The Parlement protected the instigators of the declaration through the night until they were finally taken into custody on May 6, 1788.

The king again called a lit de justice on May 8, 1788, and prior to this lit de justice, Brienne announced futher financial reforms in the press. At the ceremony of the lit de justice, the king opened with several measures intended to correct miscarriages of justice. The king then announced judicial reforms intended to support his absolute power. The parlements lost nearly all legal powers, and all were immediately sent into recess. Around the country, the lower courts, parlements and other essential offices began to refuse to function. They did not register new laws and justice came to a stop across France.

With the nobility, clergy and bourgeoisie now united in their objections to the king's actions, damage control began in the coming months. In early July, Brienne announced a call for opinions on the composition of the Estates-General, which Brienne and the king hoped would distract the population from the disliked judicial reforms and perhaps and brew dissent between various groups. The attempt failed. While there were some suggestions made for the Estates-General, poor press, including more than 500 political pamphlets, continued in earnest.

Continuing financial difficulties and impending bankruptcy led Brienne to announce, on August 8, 1788, that the Estates-General would meet on May 1, 1789, but this announcement did not improve the state of finances either. The French government was bankrupt.

Brienne was left with no other solution. As principal minister, Brienne convinced Louis XVI to recall Jacques Necker. While Necker had not been honest with the people, he nonetheless retained their favor, and after approximately one week of negotiations, Necker returned to Versailles. Necker's return was Brienne's last action in government - he resigned when Necker returned.

The Estates-General and National Assembly

When the tax reforms of Brienne were rejected by the Assembly of Notables, this body suggested instead that the king summon the Estates-General to consider the matter of economic reforms. This was a long-standing institution within the French constitution whereby the king could, if he wished, call together a conclave that represented the interests of the estates to provide advice. However, this was rarely used; in fact, when it was suggested by the Assembly of Notables as a possible way out of the impasse, the Estates-General had not been called since 1614.

For his part, Necker no longer had faith in the monarchy and expected only to provide some degree of stability until the Estates-General could meet. Necker's return to power was welcomed by the people, and he recalled the parlements, requesting that they register the meeting of the Estates-General in January 1789. The Parlement de Paris declared that the Estates-General must meet according to the "forms observed in 1614", which had provided the nobility and clergy with more power than the Third Estate, the bourgeoisie. Around the country, discussions continued, with many regions hoping for a Third Estate with twice the representation of the nobility or clergy, with votes by head. National opinion came out strongly against the form of the 1614 Estates-General. The Assemble of Notables met, but would not approve the form of the Estates-General and also aroused significant public displeasure. Their inability to achieve anything led to the postponement of the Estates-General until April or May.

Necker also eliminated many of the restrictions on the people of France. He stopped enforcing censorship regulations, allowing the free press and free circulation of ideas, and he reopened political clubs, allowing gatherings and discussions to take place. These changes helped to increase his popularity among the bourgeoisie of Paris and elsewhere. But other conditions, including natural ones, contributed to the eventual downfall of the French government. A July 1788 hailstorm in northern France destroyed crops, after a spring drought had already damaged the harvest. The coming winter was also the worst in memory. Necker immediately re-imposed controls on grain sales when he took office in late August, but his actions were, at this time, too little and too late to improve the situations of the suffering people. Grain prices were already increasing in August and continued to climb throughout the next year, adding to the collapse of the economy. No one had funds to spend, so there was no demand for consumer goods.

On December 27, 1788, Necker published a document called the "Result of the king's Council of State", the result of a week's worth of meetings with Louis XVI. While the provinces and parlements could not agree upon the composition of the Estates-General, Louis XVI agreed that the Third Estate should be doubled. Necker did not answer whether they had to vote by head or in common, opting to leave it to their own agreement. While he did not answer all questions, he largely preserved his own popularity with the "Result of the king's Council of State".

Elections took place among the clergy. While all beneficed clergy were entitled to participate, monasteries and similar foundations could send only a single representative. Each member of the landed nobility was allowed to sit in the Estates-General, so no elections were required.

Hundreds of pamphlets appeared throughout the winter months, including "What is the Third Estate?" Many of these concerned the powers of the Third Estate, strongly criticizing the privilege of the nobility and clergy. During this time, a number of leaders emerged among the Third Estate for the first time. These leaders, as well as popular publications, influenced the composition of the Third Estate during elections around France at the beginning of the year 1789.

The Third Estate did have elections. Each male taxpayer over 25 years old was allowed a vote in the primary assembly, and the primary assemblies chose two delegates for each hundred households. The Third Assembly was allowed four representatives for each two nobles and two clergy, chosen from the delegates elected in the primary assemblies. The Third Estate also produced cahiers, or lists of grievances. The cahiers drafted for the 1789 Estates-General largely reflected the desires of the revolutionary pamphlet producers.

While the government did not involve itself in the elections, the process of forming the Estates-General created an assembly of clergy largely confined to parish priests of old nobility rather than new, and courtiers faired quite poorly. The majority of those serving for the nobility were landed nobility who lived in smaller towns and had no experience with public life, barring military service. For the Third Estate, parish priests serving as the representatives was ideal, as these priests worked with the people rather than for the church hierarchy. The Third Estate was not made up of artisans, peasants or other workers, but bourgeoisie with enough leisure to engage in this slow and arduous process, including lawyers and office-holders.

There was a clear split between old nobility, those who had held high rank for at least four generations, and new nobility, many of whom had recently purchased their titles from the king. There were frequent and sometimes violent differences of opinion between the two groups. The old nobility maintained an almost medieval "even feudal sense of honor and duty"[26]. For them any change was abhorrent. Other were followers of enlightenment philosophers and much more open to reform. It wasn't unknown for political discussions between members of the nobility to end in duels, sometimes with fatal results.

The clergy did not have this kind of problem but nonetheless suffered form an inner division as well. The deputies nominated by the church to take part in the Estates-General came from both high and low clergy and it soon became apparent that the views of the two were very different.

On May 4, 1789, a procession through the streets of Paris marked the formal opening of the Estates-General. Thousands of Parisians watched as the 1,200 elected deputies marched behind the king and the Royal Family from Notre Dame cathedral to Saint Louis. It was notable that the crowds applauded and cheered the deputies of the Third Estate, clad in somber black, and the ordinary priests of the low clergy. They stayed ominously silent as the nobles and cardinals of the high clergy, dressed in opulent finery, passed by.

On May 5, in the Hall of Menus Plaisirs at the Palace of Versailles, the Estates-General was formally convoked. The opening was attended by Necker and by two men representing the Third Estate who would become important figures in what followed: Honoré Gabriel Riqueti and Emmanuel-Joseph Sieyès.

Although he was elected as a representative for the Third Estate, Honoré Gabriel Riqueti was a member of the nobility, holding the title Count of Mirabeau. However, he was committed to reform and was known as an effective speaker. Mirabeau became an important symbolic figure within the Third Estate; despite being of noble birth, he had espoused the cause of enlightenment, supporting the notion that equality really was possible, regardless of family or birth.

---

[26] Tackett, *Becoming a Revolutionary*, 137.

Mirabeau

Emmanuel-Joseph Sieyès was from a bourgeois family, though he had been disinherited by his father for his extreme views. He had initially undergone training as a priest but had combined his theological reading with avid perusal of the works of the enlightenment philosophers. He finally abandoned his training for the clergy to focus on writing political articles and pamphlets. He is credited with creating such terms "social science", "electoral system," "*ancien régime*" and "ethocracy"[27]. He had previously served on the Assembly of Notables, but by 1789 he had become well-known amongst supporters of the Third Estate for both his writing and his public speaking.

---

[27] Ibid., ix-x.

Sieyès

The first meeting of the Estates-General on May 5 heard three speeches; one by the king, one by his Minster of Justice and one by Necker as Minister of Finance. Altogether, the three speeches lasted for a little under four hours and all presented the same message: the current problems which faced France were entirely due to an economic crisis. The main issues were considering how to improve the finances of the state, how to make the payment of taxes fairer across classes and, most importantly, how to relieve the hunger that the bread price increase had caused for the poorest people. Necker's speech focused on the necessity for the nobility and the clergy to accept that they had a responsibility towards the state and that this implied the payment of the taxes from which they were currently exempt. He urged them to consider renouncing this privilege for the good of the state itself and for all the people of France.

However, these speeches also made it clear that the role expected of the Estates-General by the king was severely proscribed. While they were expected to provide advice on the solution of the economic crises, they were not to be permitted to question the system that had allowed this crisis to develop or to suggest reforms. In particular, there was to be no discussion of the role of the king, nor of the way in which France was governed.

For many of the deputies of the Third Estate, this was a crushing disappointment. Many had come to the Estates-General expecting that this was, finally, an opportunity to discuss reforms of the way in which France was governed. The opening speeches made it clear that the king was simply not willing to listen to suggestions on more effective and more representative government. He would accept only advice on how to deal with the immediate problem that the French state was close to bankruptcy.

This realization caused many deputies of the Third Estate to become intransigent. It seemed that the Estates-General was not to be what they and the mass of the French population had hoped for and expected. Many of the deputies had no interest in solving the economic crises in order to prop up what they saw as a corrupt and inefficient system of government.

After the opening speeches, the Estates-General began its deliberations the following day, 6th May. The 600 deputies of the Third Estate gathered in the main session room and waited for the representatives of the other two estates. And waited. And waited some more.

Instead of joining the Third Estate in the main session room, representatives of the clergy and the nobility met separately in their respective session rooms discussing the issue of credentials. Unlike the deputies of the Third Estate, representatives of the clergy and the nobility were not elected by popular vote, and both felt it necessary to spend time verifying the eligibility of each of their own representatives before proceeding to a general discussion with the others. Having waited in vain for most of the day for the other two Estates to join them, the members of the Third Estate "concluded that they had the full confidence of the royal government to proceed as they saw fit"[28].

On the following day, the members of the Third Estate returned to the main session chamber and once again found that they had it to themselves. The clergy and the nobles were still involved in their own heated discussions about who precisely had the right to attend the meeting. The Third Estate sent emissaries to the other two, suggesting that they might at least all convene in the same room to discuss the matter of credentials together. Neither was willing to do this, though the clergy showed at least some signs of making progress with their own discussions. This absurd situation continued for several days, with the members of the Third Estate convening in the main session room and the clergy and nobility refusing to join them until their own internal deliberations were complete.

To the members of the Third Estate, the message seemed clear that the nobility and clergy had

---

[28] Tackett, *Becoming a Revolutionary*, 122.

no real interest in taking part in a real discussion on how to alleviate the problems afflicting the majority of the French population. Instead, they were content to spend their time on what appeared from the outside to be petty squabbles. The other two seemed happy to waste time while only the "Third Estate was concerned with the affairs of the nation"[29].

Days passed and there was still no meeting of the members of all three estates. Meanwhile, the king did not want any information to filter out and placed a prohibition on the dissemination of news about what was happening in Versailles. Riqueti published a daily journal under his title as Count of Mirabeau on what was happening in the Estates-General but, on the orders of the king this was heavily censored to remove any reference to the lack of progress. Mirabeau simply changed the name of the publication and continued to provide the people of France with daily reports on progress, or rather, lack of progress[30].

The members of the Third Estate continued to meet and to hold their own debates despite the absence of the others. The main topic in the early days was whether it was better to wait for the other two to join the debate or to act on their own? There was no clear consensus, but, as the days extended into weeks, there was a growing desire to at least begin the debate. The representatives of the Third Estate repeatedly asked the clergy to join them, and by May 24 it was clear that some junior priests were willing to accept this invitation, but the senior clergy were generally not. Briefly, it seemed that the clergy might be split.

The potential defection of some of the clergy to join the Third Estate was important. There were 1,200 deputies in total, 600 from the Third Estate and 300 each from the clergy and the nobles. Traditionally, each estate had been given a single vote on all issues, and these were decided by a majority within the estates. This meant that the nobles and the clergy acting together could always defeat the Third Estate. However, one of the things that the deputies of the Third Estate had been discussing during the debates amongst their own members was a change to the voting system. It was, they decided, iniquitous that the Third Estate, representing the vast majority of French people, could be defeated in votes by the other two, who represented only a tiny fraction. They proposed that the system of voting be changed so that each deputy be given one vote. That would mean that the votes of the Third Estate would be equal to the combined votes of the nobles and clergy. This meant that if even a few members of the clergy defected, it would become possible for the Third Estate to carry votes against the wishes of the other two.

The king heard of this and quickly intervened, insisting that any debate must take place in front of his Minster of Justice. This meant that all members of each estate had to be present for the debate to be meaningful, and it stopped the junior priests from joining the members of the Third Estate in the main session room[31].

---

[29] Fitzsimmons, *The Remaking of France*, 35.

[30] Michelet, *Historia de La Revolución Francesa I*, 51.

[31] Ibid., 52.

By early June, one month after the formal start of the assembly, the situation remained unchanged and the representatives of the Third Estate were rapidly losing patience with the others. Under the leadership of Sieyès, it was agreed that Third Estate would invite the clergy and the nobility to the session hall for the last time. The invitation stipulated a period of one hour for members to appear and noted that absences would be recorded. No members of the clergy or the nobility entered the main session room within the set time. As a result, Sieyès argued that the Third Estate should proceed without the other two, reminding those present that it represented more than ninety-six percent of the total population of France and suggesting that this gave it the moral authority to continue.

In the following days, dialogue continued between the members of the Third Estate and the clergy. The attitude of some clergy was conciliatory, but they felt that they were constrained by the king's edict and could not attend a debate in the main session room unless as part of the whole body of clergy representatives. By the 17th of June, the patience of the representatives of the Third Estate finally ran out. After six weeks, they had still not been joined by a single member of the nobility or the clergy. On that day, the 600 Third Estate deputies announced that they were no longer members of the Estates-General but that they were now a National Assembly with authority to act on behalf of the people of France without the participation of the other two estates.

The members of the Third Estate also announced a change of name. Henceforth they would be known as the Commons, in order to wash "clean of old humiliation"[32]. The announcement of the National Assembly was an electrifying and radical moment. Jean Sylvain Bailly was elected president, and the new National Assembly's first edict was a reaffirmation of what Necker had said at the opening of Estates-General: the tax on the privileged classes which had previously been exempt would enter into force immediately. Its second act was to assume responsibility for the national debt, understanding itself as the state and the guarantor of it[33]. Lastly, the National Assembly appointed a commission to deal with generalized hunger.

---

[32] Furet, *The French Revolution, 1770-1814*, 63.
[33] Michelet, *Historia de La Revolución Francesa I*, 59.

Bailly

The king refused to meet with members of the Third Estate or to recognize the National Assembly. He claimed that grief over the recent death of his son made this impossible, though it was noted that he did receive visits from members of the clergy and the nobility during the same period. Either way, it was clear that the king was coming to regret his decision to convoke the Estates-General.

The Tennis Court Oath

On the morning of June 20, the members of the new National Assembly arrived to find that the Hall of *Menus-Plaisirs*, the main session room in which they had gathered until then, was locked and guarded. Officials explained that the hall was closed in order to make preparations for the visit of the king, which was scheduled on June 22.

The night before, in Marly, in a palace built by Louis XIV six kilometers north of Versailles, the king had met with his most distinguished advisers to discuss the actions of the Third Estate. What concerned him most was that it seemed possible that at least some of the clergy and perhaps even some nobles might be willing to join the Third Estate. If that happened, it would allow the Third Estate to make recommendations to the king. As one historian pointed out, "Among the clergy, where internal strife had been lively, there were only forty-six bishops out of 300 deputies, and many country priests were being attracted by their Third Estate neighbours. One third of the nobility group had been won over to liberal ideas, and was dominated by the reputation of the parlementaire Du Port and the American prestige of La Fayette.[34]"

An early 18ᵗʰ century depiction of Marly

In an effort to prevent or at least postpone this alliance, Louis XVI ordered the immediate closure of the main hall, but the members of the Third Estate were not informed and found out

---

[34] Furet, *The French Revolution, 1770-1814*, 60.

only at 7:00 a.m. the following morning, an hour prior to the scheduled start of the assembly session. They were told not by the king but in a letter written by the Marquis de Dreux-Brézé, Versailles' court master of ceremonies.

By 8:00 a.m., the deputies of the Third Estate had gathered in front of the hall doors with guards blocking the door to the meeting room. Some deputies tried to force the door open but were prevented by the guards. Undeterred, President Bailly declared the opening of the session right there in front of the door.

It quickly became obvious that it was impossible to hold a meeting of 600 people in such a confined space. At that point, Deputy Joseph-Ignace Guillotin, a statesman and ardent opponent of capital punishment who ironically became the namesake of the guillotine, suggested that they meet instead in the Royal Tennis Court of Versailles, which had been abandoned for almost 100 years. Other options were suggested, and some of these were openly rebellious, including a march to the palace at Marly where the king was at the time, or even a march through the streets of Paris, which would have almost certainly have caused a violent uprising against the monarchy[35]. Instead, they agreed to reconvene in the Royal Tennis Court, which was generally viewed as less confrontational than either marching though Paris or to Marley.

[35] Michelet, *Historia de La Revolución Francesa I*, 61.

Guillotin

The Royal Tennis Court

It is important to note that, while by agreeing to hold their meeting at the Tennis Court the deputies knew that they were going against the king's wishes, they were not at this stage anti-royalist. When, three days earlier, they became by their own authority the National Assembly, they did so while shouting, "Long live the king!"[36] Despite the preferential treatment the king showed to the other estates and his carelessness towards them, on June 20, the National Assembly was in no way hostile towards the king. Their resentment was against the nobility and what they regarded as unfair system of taxation and privilege. However, when they agreed to meet at the Royal Tennis Court, they were aware that they were acting against the wishes of the king and that it might have serious individual and collective consequences.

When they finally convened in the dilapidated indoor court, all the representatives of the Third Estate were present and had been joined by a few members of the clergy and even one or two nobles. One of the deputies, Jean-Joseph Mounier, proposed that the members of the Assembly should take an oath to continue in their work and not to separate until they had drawn up and agreed a new constitution for France. Another deputy, Jean-Baptiste-Pierre Bevière, drew up an oath.

---

[36] Ibid., 63.

Mounier

Bevière

Considering the bloody chaos and insurrection that was to follow, the oath itself seems relatively innocuous: "The National Assembly, considering that as it was called upon to determine the constitution of the kingdom, to effect the regeneration of public order, and to maintain the true principles of the monarchy, nothing can prevent that it should continue its deliberations in whatever place it is forced to establish itself, and finally that wherever its members are gathered, there sits the National Assembly; Decides that all the members of this Assembly will immediately swear a solemn oath never to separate, and to meet anywhere where circumstances may require, until such time as the constitution of the kingdom is established and strengthened on solid foundations.[37]"

President Bailly read the oath and was the first to swear on it[38]. The members of the Third Estate and those clergy and nobles present all subsequently signed and swore to the oath.

The following day, June 21, a number of nobles met with the king in the palace at Marly and warned him of the seriousness of what had happened. They urged him to take action, offering their own swords to be used against the members of the National Assembly if required.

On Monday, the 22nd, Bailly received the news that the royal session scheduled for the following day would not take place until later. When representatives arrived at Versailles, they found not only the main hall, the *Menus-Plaisirs*, locked, but also the abandoned Royal Tennis Court. The Count of Artois, a younger brother of Louis XVI who would a few decades later become a rather unpopular king himself, ordered the closing of the Royal Tennis Court because he claimed that he was about to use it to play, despite the fact it had been unused for about a century.

The assembly, without a place to meet, first asked for help from the Recoletos, a French Franciscan movement, but they were denied access to their house since they did not want to be involved in the political struggle. Finally, the National Assembly found a venue in in the Church of Saint Louis, where a number of clergy deputies to the Estates-General had been gathering since morning[39].

On June 23, just three days after taking the oath, the members of the National Assembly would face the first royal opposition. On that day, the king was to appear in front of the Estates-General at Versailles and present a speech. Given what had happened, it was inevitable that Louis XVI's speech would address the events that had taken place in the Royal Tennis Court.

The meeting began with a deliberate snub to those who had signed the oath. The king, the clergy, and the nobles were allowed to enter by the front door, which was then locked. As a result, the members of the Third Estate were forced to enter via a rear door, and many were unable to get in and remained outside in the rain[40].

The king had spent some time working on his speech. Necker drafted a moderate speech,

---

[37] Sa'adah, *The Shaping of Liberal Politics in Revolutionary France A Comparative Perspective,* 110.
[38] Michelet, *Historia de La Revolución Francesa I,* 63.
[39] Ibid., 64.
[40] Ibid., 67.

conciliatory in tone and promising at least some measure of government reform, but this was rejected in favor of a more hardline approach. The king told the packed room that any "agreements" made by the deputies of the Third Estate were invalid and had no meaning. The National Assembly would be allowed to continue to deliberate, but it was not to be permitted to discuss the privileges of the *ancien régime* or to speak of a change to a republican form of government. Appointments to all public and military positions were to continue to be exclusively in the hands of the king and the notion of freedom of speech was rejected, since this could only be allowed as long as it did not conflict with the king's wishes. The members of the Third Estate received the king's speech in utter silence. The nobility applauded and cheered loudly.

This was a pivotal moment in what would become the French Revolution. By taking the Tennis Court Oath, the members of the Third Estate and the few clergy and nobles who also signed were making clear a desire for change that also reflected strong feelings within the wider population. However, the nature of the oath demonstrated that these changes were intended to be made within the context of the continuation of the monarchy. It seems entirely possible that had the king done as Necker suggested and made concessions, a revolution might have been avoided entirely. Instead, he chose to reject them entirely, leaving those who had taken the oath only three days before with only two options: they either had to abandon their calls for change or they had to disobey their king.

Their decision became clear in minutes. The king ended his speech by telling all those present to leave and to reconvene the following day to continue the work of the Estates-General. The bulk of the clergy and nobles left, but those who had signed the oath did not. Brézé, the master of ceremonies of the court, reminded them of the king's instructions and was immediately questioned by Bailly, who responded that the National Assembly was in session and could not be separated until its end. Michelet described the scene: "In the following minutes, the Revolution found three Roman phrases to express the new era. Bailly: 'The assembled nation cannot take orders.' Sieyès: 'You are today what you were yesterday.' Mirabeau: 'We shall not leave our places save at bayonet point.'"[41] Thus, once again, the members reiterated the Tennis Court Oath.

Soon after, workers entered the room in order to clear it out. Bailly explained the situation to them and they left the room as it was, so the members of the National Assembly remained in the room, defying the king's order. Debate amongst its members became heated, as it was obvious that the king was not willing to negotiate. No solution was found, but Mirabeau called for the meeting to pass a resolution declaring that the members of the National Assembly were inviolate, threatening the death penalty to anyone who attempted to move against them.

The nobility was thrilled both by the king's speech and the reaction of the Third Estate, and they assumed the king would use the troops he had gathered outside Paris to move against them. The king, however, knew that if he chose to move against the assembly, the political cost of

---

[41] Ibid.

repression would be immense and might even trigger the open rebellion that seemed to loom on the horizon. At the same time, it was also dangerous for him to allow them to openly defy his wishes and to continue meeting out of the reach of his control.

Patriotic sentiment grew, all supporting the National Assembly, and most of the remaining clergy joined the National Assembly on the 24th of June. A significant number of the nobility also appeared at the National Hall, and on June 27, the king all but conceded by ordering the First and Second Estates to join the National Assembly. The news was well-received, and when they appeared on a balcony at Versailles, Louis XVI and his queen were cheered. Many people, including those in the National Assembly, hoped this was the beginning of a return to peace and stability.

Of course, as anyone who is the least bit familiar with the French Revolution knows, that would not be the case.

The Storming of the Bastille

An illustration depicting the Bastille and its grounds

229. Die Bastille vor ihrer Zerstörung.

A 19th century engraving depicting the Bastille

The violent days of the Hundred Years' War, when the armies of the English kings ravaged France from end to end and the blackened, skeletal wrecks of burned church spires became known as "Knolles' miters" after Sir Robert Knolles (King Edward III's brutal field commander), brought about the genesis of the citadel known to history as the Bastille. Paris' eastern gate was deemed to be poorly defended, and accordingly, a citadel of eight drum towers and connecting walls was erected to command this crucial portion of the French capital's defenses.

The compact rectangular castle emerged out of a succession of construction efforts, beginning with just two towers constructed in 1357 to protect the Porte (or gate) Saint-Antoine at the command of Etienne Marcel, Provost of Paris. This type of fortified gate was known at the time as a bastille, a term which did not apply solely to this particular entryway. However, as time went on, the generic term for the fortification type became the "given name" of the citadel into which this particular bastille (or barbican, in English) developed.

Marcel's life and death remained closely linked to the *bastille* of the Porte Saint-Antoine, coloring the fortress' earliest days with betrayal, treachery, and blood. Provost Marcel, a schemer whose own plots ultimately led to his undoing, rebelled against the French crown and, in the last days of July 1358, sought to betray the capital to the rival King of Navarre. The city, however, was loyal to King John II, the legitimate monarch of France according to the laws and customs of the day.

On July 31st, 1358, Marcel sought to open the gates to the vulture-like bands of English soldiers who were ravaging, pillaging, and burning its suburbs. He first tried to open the Porte Saint-Denis but was chased away by an armed and mounted draper, Jean Maillart, and a group of furious guardsmen. He then went to the Porte Saint-Antoine, desperate to escape the barbaric punishments which the age's cruelty would doubtless have inflicted on him if he was captured alive and turned over to King John II "the Good": "Marcel next appeared […] at the Porte St. Antoine, where he again demanded the keys and met the same response, which was led by a certain Pierre des Essars, a knighted bourgeois […] In a rush upon the Provost, the guards of St. Antoine struck him down, and when the bloodstained weapons had lifted and the melee had cleared, the body of Etienne Marcel lay trampled and dead in the street." (Tuchman, 1978, 178).

Thus, through some grim irony of history, the man who oversaw the first days of the Bastille's existence died seeking to obtain possession of its keys, a complete contrast to the fate of the Bastille's last keeper. That luckless official would perish with a carpenter's saw ripping through his neck shortly after surrendering the castle's keys for the final time.

Most castles and fortresses of the medieval period were residences as much as examples of military architecture, and when originally in use, many of these buildings had such unexpected details as colorful murals in their living spaces or tubs of roses or other flowers situated on their peacetime battlements. Many were never used as prisons, and those that were tended to be converted into places of incarceration long after the medieval era had ended. The Bastille, however, became a dungeon for political prisoners within a short while of its first stones being laid, and this role was reinforced over the centuries as Paris grew far beyond its original walls and the Bastille no longer served any defensive function. Embedded deep within the city, it became a place for storing prisoners and military supplies, both of which contributed to its eventual fate.

The Bastille came to official notice again 11 years after Etienne Marcel was chopped to pieces near it by loyal French knights and soldiers. Still in the midst of the Hundred Years' War, the English were still haunting France like an unbreakable curse, looting, raping, and committing arson in the Paris area as well as other regions. Worse, their destructive potential was augmented by bands of unemployed mercenaries, who were driven to robbery and extortion both by their lack of pay and by the unchecked power of coercion they could exert on a local level. In response, another Provost of Paris, Hugh Aubriot, received the royal command of King Charles V to greatly expand the Bastille, thus enhancing its capacity to defend the key Porte Saint-Antoine. This order was issued in 1369, and the expansion began in 1370. Building a castle was a tremendous undertaking, and the work was not completed until 1380 or perhaps even a year or two later, when a new king, Charles VI, occupied the throne of France.

Charles V of France

From a fortified gate with two towers, the Bastille grew rapidly under Hugh Aubriot's guidance. The Provost personally laid the first foundation stone of the expanded castle on April 22, 1370, clueless that the walls rising under his oversight would eventually imprison him. Within a decade, the citadel had achieved the form it possessed, with only a few slight modifications, for another 400 years until its demolition.

In this final form, the Bastille was made up of eight cylindrical drum towers arranged in two rows of four and connected by curtain walls 10 feet thick, forming an elongated, crooked rectangle in overall plan. The walls and towers stood at precisely the same height of 78 feet, providing a commanding view over the rooftops of Paris and a formidable stronghold that was difficult to assault in the days before gunpowder. The top surface of the walls and towers formed a continuous walkway around the building's summit, an unusual arrangement given that each tower in a castle was typically an isolated strongpoint to make it difficult for besiegers to carry the whole work simply by seizing one section of wall.

This unusual design was a revolutionary architectural feature at the time and was deliberately chosen by the Provost in an attempt to make the Bastille more militarily useful. For its era, this arrangement was "a most unusual feature, [with] the curtain walls […] raised to the same height as the towers so that an active defense could be conducted by rushing troops to any threatened point without their being delayed by negotiating entrances and towers blocking the way." (Anderson, 1984, 208). This fresh approach to castle architecture was imitated at Pierrefonds, Tarascon, and Nunney, and may have even inspired the low-lying artillery forts of later epochs.

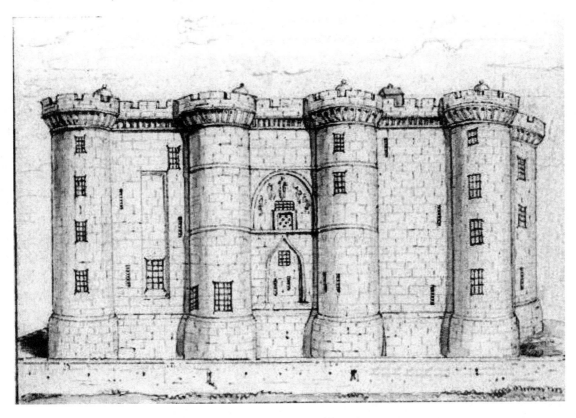

An 18th century sketch of the Bastille

The Bastille was originally fitted with four gates, with the Rue Saint-Antoine running directly through its courtyards. By the time of the French Revolution in 1789, however, three of the gates had been filled in with masonry, so only a single approach remained. This was due to the efforts of King Henry II, who had all the gates except the south gate sealed in anticipation of foreign attacks during the 1550s. Each of the towers, which were individually named after famous incidents or persons associate with them, included a vaulted "cachot" or dungeon in its foundations and living quarters in the upper floors.

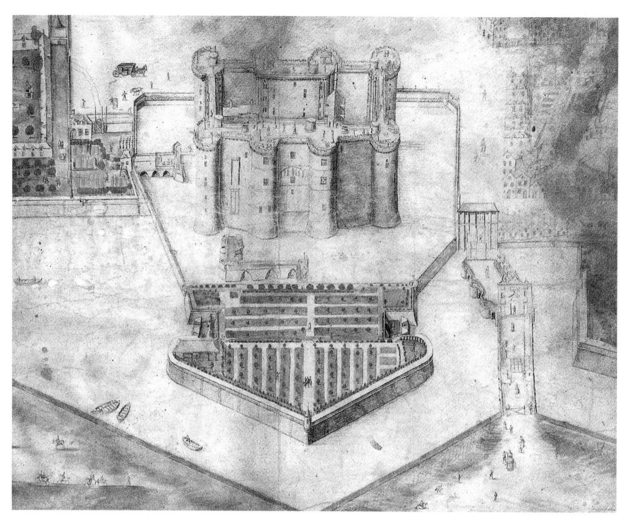

A 16th century depiction of the Bastille

From the moment of its completion, the Bastille seemed haunted by the spirit of injustice and oppression. Hugh Aubriot, the Provost of Paris who laid its foundation stone and oversaw its completion, was the first man to experience its prison cells from the inside. In 1380, Aubriot made the rather noble error of attempting to protect the city's luckless Jews from rioting Parisians. During that riot over taxes, "in a frenzy of triumph and unspent wrath, the people rushed to rob and assault the Jews, the one section of society on whom the poor could safely vent their aggression." (Tuchman, 1978, 360). Aubriot made efforts to return the goods plundered from the Jews and to restore their children to them, the latter having been kidnapped by the Parisians under pretext of converting them to Christianity, and though his attempt was only weakly successful, his reputation was tarnished in the minds of his countrymen by this act of justice and kindness. Though Aubriot "won […] the favor of the bourgeois by construction of the first sewers and by vigorous repairs of walls and bridges," trouble was brewing for the luckless official: "He was marked for destruction by the clergy, whom he openly insulted, and by the University, which he scorned as that 'nursery of priests' and whose privileges he combatted […] Aubriot's intervention in the case of the Jews gave the University its handle for revenge.

Accused of heresy, sodomy, and being a false Christian, and, specifically, of 'profaning the sanctity of baptism' by returning the Jewish children, he was brought to trial before the Bishop of Paris in May 1381. [...] he was accused of neglect of a virtuous wife, of buying virgins, and having 'recourse to sorcery that his passions might triumph,' [...] and having carnal relations with Jews. (Tuchman, 1978, 361).

This torrent of bizarre accusations would have resulted in his execution, most likely with the hideous refinements of torture which the medieval Church used freely as an instrument of ecclesiastical terror, had not the powerful Duke of Burgundy, Philip the Bold, intervened on his behalf. Aubriot's sentence was commuted to life imprisonment on a "penitential" diet of bread and water. He was first imprisoned in the Bastille, an irony which probably didn't escape him, and he was then moved to the Fort L'Eveque (Coueret, 1890, 6). The tale of the Bastille's first notable prisoner ended on a surprisingly positive note when Aubriot was soon freed from his prison by a Paris mob and wisely took to his heels, fleeing from the city to his birthplace of Dijon. There he lived until he died of natural causes, either in the following year (1382) or, more likely, in 1391, retaining his liberty to the end.

The Bastille continued to see more use as a prison than as a military installation after Aubriot's fortunate escape. King Charles VII declared the castle to be a royal prison in 1417, and when King Henry V of England, Shakespeare's "lovely bully," seized Paris in 1420, he used the Bastille both as a citadel to dominate the metropolis and as a dungeon for his French enemies. This continued until the English were evicted from the city in 1436.

King Louis XI of France, dubbed "the Universal Spider" by his enemies because of his cunning, patience, and cruelty, further darkened the reputation of the Bastille by continuing its use as a place of incarceration. Louis seemed to relish keeping his political enemies alive for years exposed in small cages, and, if the chroniclers are to be believed, used the Bastille as a place not merely of confinement but of sadistic torture as well: "The dungeons under the towers are filled with a mud which exhales the most offensive scent. They are the resort of toads, newts, rats, and spiders. It was in these dungeons that the tyrant Louis XI confined those he was desirous of destroying by protracted sufferings as the Princes of Armagnac, who were buried in these dungeons in holes wrought in the masonry […] and were, besides, taken out twice a week to be scourged […] and every three months to have a tooth pulled out." (Du Perray, 1774, 5).

King Louis XI

Given that the Enlightenment had penetrated even to the last of the Bourbon monarchs, and the Bastille was considerably reformed by the time of the storming on July 14th, 1789, many people have doubted the tales of horror associated with it. However, the fact that relatively civilized late 18th-century monarchs ensured that the Bastille was clean, that prisoners were given food and drink of decent quality, and that reasonable furniture and even books and some outdoor exercise were provided does not mean that every previous era was the same. There is almost a sense of eagerness on the part of some historians to whitewash the earlier periods of history, just as some seek to blacken those periods with a Gothic gloom that did not exist in reality either.

In fact, the authorities of the medieval era and Renaissance were very apt to conflate the idea of justice with the extraction of maximum suffering, physical pain, fear, and death from those who stood accused of various crimes. Though many people, if not most, lived free from direct affliction by their overlords during the period, there seems little reason to doubt that the sinister reputation of the Bastille was founded on centuries of very real deprivation, torture, despair, and cruelty committed within its walls. Indeed, the loyal servant and clear-eyed chronicler of Louis XI's reign, Phillipe de Commynes, was an early rationalist and an apparently sober historian who seems to have reported even his own failures accurately in his memoirs. Though there is always possible that the accusations were fabricated to discredit a rival, Commynes states that the governor of the Bastille, Tristan L'Hermite ("Tristan the Hermit"), considered himself judge, jury, and executioner. The medieval writer, soldier, and politician asserted that approximately 4,000 people were executed in the Bastille at the orders of Louis XI and under the supervision of Tristan L'Hermite. Some of the methods he used were impalement on spiked wheels, drowning by tying a stone around the neck and immersion of the victim's head in water, or smothering. Thousands of others were likely imprisoned for a time and then released when their political significance or the king's wrath faded, but these individuals may or may not have been tortured or mutilated in the meantime.

Though many grotesque and absurd rumors attached themselves to Louis XI and demonized the French monarch until he was viewed as an unrealistic caricature during the 18th and 19th centuries, there is no doubt whatsoever that the "Universal Spider" converted a number of castles into prisons, installed cages in them, and made no secret of the fact that he would expose even the wives of his enemies to a lingering public death in cages hung from various city gates. The testimony of Commynes, who was an ally, servant, and near-friend of the King, as well as an accurate and probably honest observer, is particularly damning in this regard. Though Louis undertook various works to benefit France and was sometimes personally generous to people who gained his notice, he did have a dark side in his dealings with political adversaries. When given power over such people, Louis XI frequently demonstrated a sadism chillingly reminiscent of later dictators who dealt with groups of people they deemed undesirable.

That said, most of the horrors committed at the Bastille seemingly did occur during the reign of King Louis XI. In the succeeding centuries, it still hosted prisoners and the occasional execution, but nowhere near the same scale. The main uptick in prisoners during these 300 years occurred during the days of King Louis XIII, thanks mostly to one of France's most famous political ministers. Cardinal Richelieu was a vindictive man with many enemies, and some of them found their way into the Bastille. After the death of this keen-minded but relentless prelate, the prison returned to relative quiescence.

Richelieu

This history is important to the fate of the Bastille, however, because it explains why the building was so strongly despised by the populace. It had always been resented to some degree as an instrument of royal domination over the Paris commune, particularly once the threat of English marauders had faded, but King Louis XI's brutality infused it with a permanent aura of pain, cruelty, and death, even in the far milder days that were to follow. A Soviet gulag or a Nazi Todeslager would retain a similar reputation even if it was used centuries afterward as a very ordinary prison, and the brief actuality of horror at the Bastille during Louis XI's reign stamped it forever with an ominous status.

Even when it no longer resembled its former self and was on the verge of being reformed out of existence as an expensive relic of an earlier era, the Bastille would prove to be a potent negative symbol that rallied the French revolutionaries who sought to overthrow the monarchy. Indeed, concealed behind a grim fog of half-remembered history and recent exaggeration, the Bastille was perhaps the building most associated with every grand and petty oppression practiced by the *Ancien Regime*.

18th century illustrations of the Bastille and Porte Saint-Antoine

A depiction of prisoners exercising in the Bastille's courtyard

The Bastille was still in full operation when the weakness of Louis XVI's government, catastrophically poor harvests, and the example provided by the American Revolution prompted the French people to protest. Revolutionary propaganda portrayed the prison as being every bit as horrific as it had been in the days of King Louis XI, and perhaps worse. Oceans of fevered prose issued from the presses of indignant patriots, making the atmosphere even more contentious.

At this point, the Bastille possessed its own species of rational grimness, but it no longer consisted of stinking muck-filled oubliettes, the agonies of flesh torn by red-hot pincers, or executions. Instead, the prison operated to dehumanize those placed in its cells with a sort of inexorable gentleness. The prisoners were held in relative comfort and were not beaten, tortured, or abused. Food was provided in sufficient amount and quality to keep the inmates healthy, and they were even allowed to walk in the inner courtyard for exercise and fresh air.

Instead, anonymity and secrecy were the instruments of state repression. Prisoners were held incommunicado, unable in many cases to inform their friends or family what had become of them. Each prisoner was kept alone and not permitted contact with the other inmates, and records were secret and sealed, so the prisoners were not told how long they would be kept within the walls. There were no hearings and no appeals or petition process. Thus, the Bastille had become a limbo of stone, , and while the inmates were physically comfortable and even enjoyed some remarkable amenities, they might as well have been marooned on a distant island. "In some of its most powerful passages, Linguet['s book] represented captivity as death, all the worse for the officially extinguished person being fully conscious of his own obliteration." (Schama, 1989, 306).

Individuals consigned to the Bastille were usually sent there as a result of a "lettre de cachet," or "letter under seal," which bore the seal impression of the King's signet ring. These letters overrode all laws and were not subject to any process of appeal. Lettres de cachet were used for many different purposes, but their most famous application was in their widespread role of royal arrest warranty. A lettre de cachet was signed and sealed by the King and countersigned by a minister of state, who had no function in the process other than witnessing that the legal instrument did, indeed, come from the King's hand and not that of a bold forger. Agents of the Crown would then find and apprehend the person named in the lettre and convey them to Bastille, frequently under cover of night to maintain maximum secrecy. Since most people could be found at home during the night, such an arrangement also made it easier to locate the target of arrest without a lengthy search.

Though the issue of the lettres de cachet was arbitrary in the sense that there was no review process and no appeal, they were not utilized for random arrests merely to instill dread and submission in the populace. Typically, the target of a lettre de cachet was someone who had come to the attention of the authorities for one of several possible reasons: "[M]ost, though not all, of [the Bastille's] prisoners were detained by *lettres de cachet* at the express warrant of the King and without any kind of judicial process. From the beginning, many of them were high-born: conspirators against the crown […] others were religious prisoners […] There were two other important categories of detainees. The first were (*sic*) writers whose works were declared seditious […] the second were delinquents, usually young, whose families had petitioned the King for their incarceration." (Schama, 1989, 303).

Towards the end of the Bastille's existence, the King of France had, in short, become something of a glorified nanny for young aristocrats, temporarily locking up rebellious teenagers until they agreed to submit to the will of their parents again. The prison's change from a true instrument of state oppression was underlined by the fact that the tiny handful of prisoners liberated during the storming of the Bastille were mostly knaves or madmen.

One great boon for those imprisoned in the Bastille during the twilight of the Bourbons was the abandonment of the subterranean cachots located in the foundation of each tower. Louis XI had made use of these loathsome pits as a form of torture, imprisoning his enemies in the stinking, slime-filled darkness crawling with various types of vermin, but the enlightened despots of the 18th century were not prepared to keep prisoners, even bitter enemies, in such conditions. Accordingly, nobody had actually been placed in the horrific cachots or oubliettes during Louis XVI's reign, despite their appearance in many melodramatic novels of the era.

A second set of chambers lay directly under the flat stone roof of the fortress and were known as "calottes." These prison chambers were still technically in use during the reign of Louis XVI, and they offered highly unpleasant conditions of their own. With low roofs that forced prisoners to walk hunched over or strike their heads on the masonry, as well as intense extremes of heat and cold over the course of the year, they were less brutal than the cachots but only in relative terms. "There is scarcely room for a bed from one arcade to another. The distance of the window from its interior aperture is the whole thickness of the wall; about ten feet. […] The Calottes have but little light. In summer, their heat is excessive; and in winter, their cold is insupportable." (Du Perray, 1774, 6).

However, the calottes were seldom or never used by the time of Louis XVI's reign, despite the fact that their use was not officially abandoned as was the case with the underground vaults. Instead, the majority of inmates were housed in the regular levels of the towers, which were quite abundant, and given that it was rare for even a dozen detainees to be present in the fortress at one time, it was never overcrowded. Each prisoner had a room to themselves which consisted of one entire floor of the tower, so the conditions were Spartan but hardly tortuous: "Most prisoners were held in octagonal rooms, about sixteen feet in diameter, in middle levels of the five- to seven-storied towers. Under Louis XVI they each had a bed with green serge curtains, one or two tables and several chairs. All had a stove or chimney […] Many [prisoners] were permitted to bring in their own possessions and to keep dogs or cats." (Schama, 1989, 304).

The tower rooms had originally been designed as living quarters for the garrison, back in the days when Hugh Aubriot thought that he was overseeing the construction of a military installation rather than a prison. As such, they even had windows, which were typically accessible via three wooden steps mounted against the inner wall. "The lower chambers look only on the ditches. […] The least disagreeable chambers have views of the country, of Paris, and of the ramparts. Although the windows of these chambers are double-grated, they are sufficiently light, as their apertures enlarge on the inside." (Du Perray, 1774, 7).

Each prisoner was allowed a stipend from which their food and other necessities were purchased, and it was higher than the average wage of a free laborer. Of course, the prison officials skimmed some of this money off the top, but since none of the literate, articulate, and indignant men who were imprisoned in the Bastille and who wrote fulminations against the crown afterward ever stated that they were in danger of starvation or were dressed in rags, enough of the money was left over following the inevitable theft by the jailers to maintain at least some semblance of normal life. Moreover, the prisoners were permitted writing materials, though they could not send or receive letters unless they could bribe a guard or smuggle a message out. They were also allowed access to the Bastille library, which consisted of several hundred volumes, mostly donated by the King. In good weather, they were allowed to walk in the courtyard for a brief time each day, under the supervision of a guard, in order to obtain light, exercise, and fresh air.

The typical term of imprisonment in the Bastille was just two months, though of course, some of the prisoners were held there temporarily before being moved to a different prison where conditions were likely to be far worse. Others remained in the Bastille for years, depending on the nature of their offenses, but the great majority, however, were released relatively quickly. If anything, the experience mostly served as an unspoken threat of how easily the King could make them disappear.

Du Perray went into considerable detail on the food that was provided to the prisoners. Though he used various adjectives to attempt to make the fare sound worse (for example, describing a chicken as "consumptive" – i.e. tubercular), the food was still likely better than that available to many working poor in Paris at the time. The prison staff apparently served two meals per day, and on most days, the morning meal consisted of soup, fish, and two entrees, while the evening meal was a dish of eggs and a plate of vegetables. Several days a week were "meat days," when the morning meal consisted of soup, bouillon, and an entree, and the evening meal consisted of roast meat, a salad, and a "ragout." Extra meat was served on Sundays. The historian Jean-Francois Marmontel, who was placed in the Bastille briefly, recalled that he enjoyed "a bottle of old Burgundy and the best mocha coffee" while behind the prison's walls, along with a variety of fresh fruits and plump chickens.

As a result, while it can't be compared with liberty, confinement in the Bastille was not a particularly dreadful fate in 18th century France in terms of physical discomfort, danger, or abuse. In some ways, the prisoners were more comfortable than those in many 21st century prisons, particularly when it came to enjoying relatively spacious private quarters. The revolutionaries, of course, would paint a very different picture in the purple prose they used when describing the Bastille, but even they seemed baffled at times by the lack of actual evidence for abuse and torture.

Among the many ironies of the French Revolution, an event which seesawed between lofty struggle and blood-drenched farce, was that the royal government itself was strongly contemplating the abolition and demolition of the Bastille. Given that the Bastille's destruction had been seriously debated in government circles for over a decade, it is even possible that the idea of leveling it originated with official plans and filtered into the popular imagination from there. In fact, reformers tackled the Bastille and its system from several directions, and had these measures been publicized, they might have deflated the histrionic propaganda of the revolutionary faction regarding both royal arrests and the Bastille itself. However, the French crown, once again proving to be its own worst enemy, kept these measures and ideas wrapped in secrecy, meaning that the improvements had no power to sway public opinion and thus did not aid the Bourbons in the escalating propaganda war leading up to the French Revolution.

One such reformer was Louis Auguste le Tonnelier, Baron de Breteuil, who was named to several high offices in the last days of the *Ancien Regime*, including the key position of Secretary of State of the Maison du Roi. Breteuil "was a high-handed reformer, a patrician large in gesture" who "set about regulating the employment of the arbitrary *lettres de cachet* that came under his jurisdiction." (Gillispie, 1980, 247). The lettres, starting in 1783, were now legally obliged to carry two vital pieces of information that were omitted up until that time: the crime for which the target of the lettre was being arrested and the exact duration of their Bastille imprisonment.

Meanwhile, the powerful finance minister Jacques Necker, who was for a time the darling of the Paris mob, suggested that the Bastille should be closed due to its enormous cost of 127,000 livres per year, which was equivalent to the income of 420 ordinary French people (Funck-Brentano, 1899, 81). Considering that the prison seldom contained more than 7 to 10 prisoners, this figure must have been fairly persuasive, and since the royal government was feeling a financial pinch and taxes were resented to the point of bringing about a revolution, Necker was probably correct in his assessment.

Several individuals and bodies, including a prominent architect named Alexandre Brogniard, one Puget of the Bastille garrison itself, and the Royal Academy of Architecture all urged that the Bastille be demolished. Some of these proposed that a public space be substituted for it, including designs with picturesque rows of columns known as colonnades, or with a triumphal pillar proclaiming King Louis XVI's dedication to the cause of liberty. Others who were more pragmatic thought that the valuable urban land the Bastille stood on should be sold off to put several million livres into the crown's coffers and partly offset the previous expenses incurred.

These suggestions were actually being mulled by the royal government in 1789, but no action was ever taken on any of them, leading to one of the most famous events in French history.

Meanwhile, the French military at the time was riddled with disloyalty due to the abhorrent treatment its members suffered. Viewed as worthless scum by society at large, their officers, and the Crown, the ordinary French soldiers were paid poorly (when they were paid at all) and were kept in line chiefly through humiliating corporal punishments. Adding insult to injury, the officer corps was largely staffed by aristocrats, so even brave, intelligent, and successful soldiers from the ordinary ranks were usually unable to rise in the military hierarchy, however much they merited it. It goes without saying that due to these factors, French regular troops were very poorly motivated and of low quality. Only the desperate would join an organization where they were treated as near-criminals both by those employing them and those protected by them, subject to arbitrary beatings if they grumbled, and paid very little and seldom on time. Desertion rates were massive (at around 3,000 men annually, or nearly the strength of a full regiment).

Given this situation, the French monarchy began to rely on foreign soldiers to maintain its position in society, a profoundly ominous development. The ordinary people hated the foreign troops, the regular French soldiers resented them as an insult to their own loyalty, and the foreigners were less than willing to perform feats of death-defying heroism for a king who wasn't their own. Any government which fears and distrusts its people so deeply that it leans on foreign military units for survival is obviously in a very tenuous situation.

Crucial to the action were the Gardes Francaises, an elite unit which was supposed to be the bodyguard of the King. King Charles IX of France, notorious for the St. Bartholomew's Day Massacre of French Protestants (Huguenots), formed the Gardes Francaises in 1563, and by 1789, these men comprised six battalions of 600 men each. During the outbreak of fighting during July 1789, only one battalion would remain loyal to the crown, while the other five battalions, consisting of about 3,000 men, joined with the Jacobin cause and became the core of the Revolutionary National Guard.

As a result, on the fateful day of the storming, the Bastille was mostly defended by a mix of "Invalides," or pensioners, and a number of Swiss grenadiers belonging to the Salis-Samade regiment. Hungarian Hussars and German Dragoons were in the area as well, and various other royal military units were in or near Paris at the time of the Bastille's fall.

The title page of Bucquoy's *Die Bastille oder die Hölle der Lebenden* depicts dragons destroying the Bastille.

Necker's immense popularity was highlighted constantly in effusive, flowery praise from all quarters. One bizarre incident served to underline the sanctity in which the Director General of Finance was held. On July 9th, a portrait of the Swiss minister was displayed at the Palais-Royal for admiration by the general public, and an aristocratic woman made the error of approaching the portrait and spitting on the face of Necker's painted likeness. She was immediately seized by three men, her skirts were lifted to expose her bare buttocks, and she was given a humiliating public spanking commemorated in a popular print of the time (Schama, 1980, 291).

At this juncture, with Necker regarded in terms of near worship by the majority of ordinary

French people, King Louis XVI decided to cashier the popular minister. With an almost sublime sense of how to best infuriate his subjects, the stout monarch resolved to assert himself at precisely the wrong moment after remaining supine for months in the face of gathering revolution. "He had had, it seems, enough of being told what was good for him and for the monarchy. His exasperation with Necker's self-righteousness had grown into something close to detestation when he had been upstaged by the Minister [...] At some point in his pursuit of boar, bird and roebuck, which continued unabated, Louis XVI had decided to assert the honor of the Bourbons (Schama, 1980, 294-295).

Having decided to take this disastrous step, Louis put the finishing touches on the mistake by dispensing with Necker's services in the most underhanded, furtive manner possible: "On Saturday the eleventh, the Minister was about to begin a congenial dinner […] when the Minister of the Navy […] arrived with a letter from the King. It was terse and to the point. It required Necker to remove himself […] – in secret – from Versailles, indeed from France altogether, and return to Switzerland." (Schama, 1980, 295).

Stoically, Necker obeyed the command of his king, calling for his coach and leaving in the darkness with his wife without even waiting to finish his meal, but his quiet departure was the spark in a political powder keg. The Swiss minister's banishment was discovered almost immediately, and on July 12th, the city erupted into a tapestry of riot, arson, raging, howling mobs, looting, and occasional brief combats.

Vast throngs, filled with rage and fear, began to gather at key points, such as the popular gathering point of the Palais-Royal, and since the people of Paris feared that the approximately 20,000 royal soldiers in the city would be set loose on them, they decided to take preemptive action. The revolutionary firebrand and journalist Camille Desmoulins provided them with a focus when he made a brief but impassioned speech to the tumultuous horde, pistol in hand: "Citizens, there is no time to lose; the dismissal of Necker is the knell of a Saint Bartholomew for patriots! This very night all the Swiss and German battalions will leave the Champ de Mars to massacre us all; one resource is left; to take arms!" (Mignet, 1826).

Desmoulins

The pace of events quickened from this point forward. Desmoulins suggested that the crowd put cockades in their hats to provide identification, and green was chosen as "the color of hope." Thousands of people tore twigs from the nearby chestnut trees and thrust the leaves into their hats as an identifying badge. They then went to the home of a sculptor identified as Curtius, where they obtained a marble bust of Necker, draped it in black cloth, and began a solemn funeral procession through the city as if mourning the death of their banished hero.

After some time, the Prince de Lambesc intercepted this relatively peaceful demonstration with his regiment of dragoons. The leader of this cavalry unit decided to attack, and his soldiers obeyed the command to charge. "The prince de Lambesc, at the head of his horsemen, with drawn sabre pursues them into the gardens, and charges an unarmed multitude who were peaceably promenading and had nothing to do with the procession. In this attack an old man is wounded by a sabre cut; the mob defend themselves with the seats, and rush to the terraces; indignation becomes general; the cry To arms! soon resounds on every side." (Mignet, 1826).

It is possible that de Lambesc's dragoons could have carried the day if not for a fatal decision on the Prince's part. He had noted several of the Gardes Francaises in the throng carrying the bust of Necker in a mock funeral procession, and accordingly, he detached 60 dragoons to the Gardes Francaises' barracks with orders to deploy in front of it and keep the Gardes imprisoned within. However, this slur on their already shaky loyalty insulted and enraged the Gardes. Filled with aggression, the elite soldiers poured from the barracks gate and drew up in fighting array facing the Prince's severely outnumbered dragoons. A shouted challenge from the Gardes' ranks warned of what was to follow: "'Qui vive?'—'Royal-allemand.'—'Are you for the third estate?' 'We are for those who command us.' Then the French guards fired on them, killed two of their men, wounded three, and put the rest to flight. They then advanced at quick time and with fixed bayonets to the Place Louis XV. and took their stand between the Tuileries and the Champs Élysées, the people and the troops, and kept that post during the night." (Mignet, 1826).

It is arguable that the monarchist cause had been lost at this moment. The most elite regiment in France, the household soldiers of the Gardes Francaises, were in open revolt against the government and were supporting the people. The Swiss soldiers encamped on the Champ de Mars advanced against the Gardes, but they were ordered not to fire by their officers. The Gardes showed no such hesitation and met the royal troops with a ferocious blast of musketry, upon which the soldiers retired to their camp again.

Though this is frequently overlooked by popular historians and novelists, the popular uprising that culminated in the fall of the Bastille had a very martial character thanks to the defection of the Gardes Francaises. Looting, pillaging, arson, and murder occurred, but there was also considerable organized activity, and the people recognized that if they did not arm themselves, they would sooner or later be crushed by the royalists' military forces. Accordingly, July 13th and July 14th were spent in a quest for weapons and powder, all while the Gardes patrolled and acted as sentinels.

Several officials sent the mobs of rebellious citizens chasing futilely about the city by pretending that muskets were hidden in various remote locations, but the Invalides, a hospital for military pensioners, contained a store of 28,000 muskets in its cellars. A man named de Sombreuil was in charge of the Invalides, and though he made an attempt to destroy these weapons on July 13, the pensioners sympathized with the people and purposely botched the job. As one historian noted, de Sombreuil "ordered twenty pensioners to take out the ramrods and unscrew the locks of these weapons; but in six hours only twenty had been disarmed. The spirit of sedition had invaded the Invalides." (Bingham, 1901, Chapter 9).

Though de Sombreuil had delayed the inevitable by a day, the royal forces in the city remained inert. Infuriated by the tricks de Sombreuil had played to keep them from arming themselves, the people returned on the morning of July 14th, accompanied by a number of Gardes Francaises. The Parisians were at the doors at first light, demanding the weapons they now knew were concealed within the Invalides, and even though de Sombreuil had the gates of the Invalides closed and barred, the pensioners took matters into their own hands. These worn-out soldiers of the king opened the Invalides' doors, and in a few minutes, the mob and their Gardes allies had made themselves masters of the building. With that, the muskets were located and distributed.

The mob was well on its way to becoming an army, but it still needed more powder to stand up to regular troops on anything like equal footing. It was known that 20,000 pounds of powder were being stored in the Bastille, which would be sufficient to arm the throngs of rebelling citizens for the foreseeable future. Accordingly, the 400-year-old castle was chosen as the next objective of both the ordinary citizens and the Gardes Francaises.

Claude Cholat's painting of the crowd gathering around the Bastille

On July 14, 1789, two men were in command of the small forcing defending the Bastille. The governor of the fortress, who held overall command, was 49 year old Bernard Rene Jourdan, Marquis de Launay. He was the son of one of the Bastille's previous governors and had actually been born inside the Bastille's walls. He had become the governor himself in 1776, 13 years prior to the Revolution, by purchasing the governorship from the incumbent. Ironically, prior to buying the office, he had been a member of the Gardes Francaises.

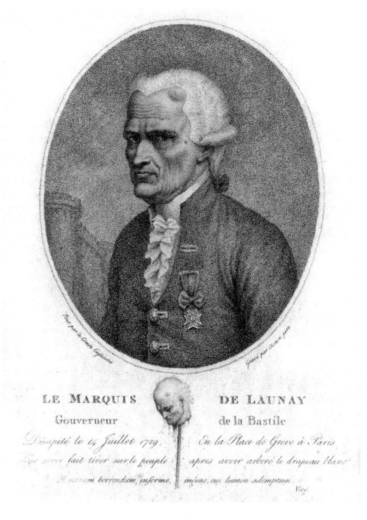

Marquis de Launay

The other main officer on the scene that day was a Swiss man, Louis de la Flue. De la Flue was a Lieutenant in the Salis-Samade regiment, which was stationed on the Champ de Mars along with the hussars from Hungary and the Prince de Lambasc's Royal-Allemand dragoons. On July 7th, the Swiss lieutenant had been detached from the regiment with 32 men, who were ordered to reinforce the Bastille. Royal forces were moving into the city at that time and some kind of fighting was clearly anticipated. De la Flue left a detailed eyewitness report on the storming of the Bastille that filled in many details which would otherwise have been lost, and he described the days leading up to the event:

> "Having received orders from the baron de Bezenval, I left on 7 July at 2 in the morning with a detachment of 32 men . . . we crossed Paris without difficulty and arrived at the Bastille where I entered with my troops. . . . During my next few days there, the Governor showed me around the place, the spots he thought the strongest and those the weakest. He showed me all the precautions that he had taken. . . He complained of the small size of his garrison and of the impossibility of

guarding the place if attacked. I told him his fears were unfounded, that the place was well fortified and that the garrison was sufficient if each would do his duty to defend it. . . .

The 12th of July we learned in the Bastille that there was the possibility of an attack on the gunpowder in the Arsenal . . . Consequently, that night a detachment transported the powder to the Bastille where it was placed in the wells, poorly covered. That same night the governor ordered the troops to remain inside the chateau, not wanting to have to defend the exterior in case of an attack.

During the day of the 13th, from the high towers of the Bastille, various fires were seen burning around the city, and we feared something similar near us, which would endanger the powder in the Bastille . . . We learned the same day from some of the citizenry of the neighborhood that they were alarmed to see canons trained on the city and we learned at the same time that the National Guard was being mobilized to defend the city. Hearing this news, the Governor ordered . . . the fortress be sealed off."

As a result, the garrison of the Bastille consisted of de la Flue's 32 Swiss soldiers and a body of "invalides," a unit of armed military pensioners whose fighting days were long behind them. There were somewhere between 80 and 115 of these men, depending on the account, so de Launay had somewhere between 112 and 147 soldiers at his command, with most of them being of very dubious quality. He also had four cannons which were actually usable, and 11 mounted on the high battlements that only fired harmless salutes.

Naturally, de Launay and de la Flue could not overlook the gathering storm in the city and thus made preparations for being attacked. The governor was nervous over the outcome, while the Swiss lieutenant remained cool and confident. Among the precautions which they took were the placement of their four usable artillery pieces in the courtyard, the positioning of a large supply of paving stones on the battlements (where they could be hurled down on any attackers), and creating new loopholes for musketry where they deemed this advisable. The 20,000 pounds of powder which had recently been placed in the Bastille were naturally prominent in their thoughts, as this trove was likely to prove a lure for any concerted anti-government rising. Armed citizens would doubtless attempt to gain possession of the powder by any means at their disposal, meaning that a sharp attack was inevitable if the city rose against the royalists.

At the same time, the gunpowder was a massive, highly volatile ammunition dump which imperiled the garrison, the Bastille, and the surrounding Faubourg Saint-Antoine. If a spark were to reach the powder, the Bastille would likely be leveled, possibly killing everyone inside and setting fire to significant portions of the adjacent Faubourg as well. A heavy responsibility lay on the shoulders of the two royal officers and their oddly-assorted command.

Despite all their efforts, the garrison was well aware that withstanding a prolonged siege would be impossible. There was no internal water supply in the Bastille at that point in time, and as de la Flue reported, "my detachment had bread for only two days and meat for only one. The pensioners had no kind of provisions." (Bingham, 1901, 273). If invested, the defenders could only hope that royal troops would move to their aid almost immediately, and if they didn't receive that help, they would be forced to capitulate within a few days at most in order to avoid dying of thirst.

De la Flue mentioned his worries about fire spreading to the powder that originally stood in the courtyard, and this was no idle fear. A large fire creates powerful updrafts that can carry pieces of burning debris high into the air, and if a piece of burning material lofted over the Bastille's 78 foot walls, an apocalyptic detonation might follow. Accordingly, much of the 13th was spent by the garrison transferring the powder kegs underground, where they were stored in the fortress' cellars.

All of the powder was safely in the vaults by dawn on July 14, but trouble began almost as soon as the sun was up that morning. Representatives of the local people approached to tell de Launay that they were attempting to keep the peace but that the sight of the Bastille's cannons were causing anxiety and panic among the population at large. Whether this was an accurate description of the popular mood or simply a ruse to attempt to persuade de Launay to stand down is unknown, but in either case, the cannons referred to were purely ceremonial pieces used for salutes, so the governor had nothing to lose by complying with the request to remove them. Thus, the 11 ceremonial guns were rolled out of sight and their embrasures were closed with timber.

This bought an hour or two of relative quiet, during which time de Launay paced up and down the main courtyard of the Bastille swinging his sword-cane nervously. Since soldiers look to their officers for reassurance in a crisis, this jittery behavior on de Launay's part could hardly have improved the morale of his troops.

Things only got worse as noon approached. Around that time, a group of citizens carrying muskets walked up to the Bastille gate. They asked for a parley, and after de Launay spoke with them for a few minutes, he allowed one of them, a Monsieur de Corny, to come inside. An impromptu conference was called, which involved de Launay, de Corny, and de la Flue, and the representative of the revolutionaries of the Faubourg Saint-Antoine lost no time in coming to the point. De la Flue noted that "this citizen demanded [...]that the guns should be removed from the towers; that in the event of the Bastille being attacked, no resistance should be offered, because we ought not to make war against the nation; that it would be useless to shed the blood of citizens […] The Governor replied that he could not surrender the Bastille to any one." (Bingham, 1901, 276).

The revolutionary leadership of the area in the Hotel de Ville actually decided not to attack the Bastille that day, but their messengers were slowed to a crawl by the dense throngs packing the streets. Before their decision could be communicated to the people, some of them had already taken matters into their own hands and were beginning an assault on the fortress.

At first, these attackers faced a series of courtyards, each one separated from the next by a drawbridge, and this initial group consisted almost entirely of armed citizens carrying muskets taken from the Invalides, hunting firearms, or even just pikes or swords. Very few Gardes Francaises were present at this point, far too few to make a significant difference, but the crowd advanced purposefully and found the first drawbridge open, giving them access to a small outer courtyard. Only one pensioner was on guard here, and since de Launay had ordered him disarmed in an effort to prevent an incident of violence, his only available action was to shout a warning in the moment or two before he was taken prisoner.

The drawbridge to the first courtyard was already down, and the rioters ensured that it remained open by hacking through its chains with the axes they had brought. This made it impossible to raise the bridge until new chains or ropes were fitted to it, but the soldiers inside continued to hold their fire, obeying the governor's orders. Meeting with no resistance, the crowd pushed forward to the second drawbridge, which opened into a courtyard known as the Governor's Courtyard.

The second gate fell as the crowd hacked their way through it with hatchets and axes, after which they entered the second courtyard, but as they advanced towards the third drawbridge, de Launay appeared on the battlements above them, which momentarily halted them. 30 men were drawn up near him on the Bastille's roof, muskets loaded and aimed at the throng. De Launay shouted to the rioters asking what they wanted, and their response was a shouted demand: "Lower the drawbridges!" De Launay declined to do so and told the crowd that they must either withdraw or be fired upon. Filled with revolutionary zeal and the need to obtain powder, the crowd started forward with their hatchets at the ready. At this moment, de Launay shouted the order to fire. The muskets of the men on the roof roared and jetted smoke, and another fusillade burst from the loopholes that had been prepared on either side of the drawbridge into the third courtyard.

The heavy lead musket balls ripped through clothing to punch holes in the flesh, organs, and bones of people beneath. Screaming rioters fell to the courtyard's paving stones, wounded or dying after their bodies were punctured by the defenders' shots, and the shocking scene momentarily dismayed the Parisian mob, which surged back but then gathered fresh aggression and charged forward. Some in the mob discharged their weapons at men on the roof or at those hidden behind the loopholes in the wall.

The second charge was met with another blistering volley of musket fire, and this time the crowd fled farther, leaving the second courtyard dotted with corpses. The retreat caused a lull in the fighting, and at this juncture, de la Flue took steps to make the third drawbridge even more formidable. He took a section of 10 men and placed them directly in front of the bridge, and he even joined them to bolster their resolve. He also had two holes cut in the drawbridge, making improvised ports through which two of the garrison's four cannon could fire.

Charles Thévenin's painting depicting the storming of the Bastille

Meanwhile, the crowd temporarily abandoned the Bastille and gathered at the Place de Greve, a square often used for public executions during the *Ancien Regime*. They were frustrated and infuriated by their failure, and they nearly took out their frustrations by murdering the revolutionary Committee in the Hotel de Ville. However, events were about to take a more ominous turn for the Bastille's garrison, starting a sequence of actions that would lead to de Launay's unconditional surrender.

The sound of gunfire had attracted the notice of the Gardes Francaises, and at approximately 3:00 p.m., 300 Gardes appeared in the street near the Bastille, led by a second lieutenant. Somewhere between 300 and 600 armed citizens accompanied them. The revolutionaries later drew up a list of 954 "Conquerors" who were supposed to have taken part in the second phase of the Storming, but most historians now believe that the force – a curious amalgam of elite professional soldiers and bloodthirsty amateurs – numbered several hundred less.

Though unruly and chaotic due to the large number of armed civilians present, the new contingent of revolutionary besiegers was commanded to some effect by two men. One of these was Second Lieutenant Jacob Elie of the Gardes Francaises, promoted to Major General by Napoleon before dying at the age of 79 in 1825. The other was Pierre-Augustin Hulin, a former sergeant of the Gardes Francaises who was also destined to become a Major General under Napoleon. This pair proved instrumental in the Bastille's fall by coordinating the efforts of the Gardes Francaises with the armed civilians who made up the bulk of the "Conquerors."

In addition to at least 600 musketeers, the fresh force of attackers dragged two pieces of artillery with them, and one of these was a ceremonial piece which the overlord of Siam had sent to King Louis XIV, the famous Sun King, several generations earlier. As one writer noted, "With them were two cannon, one bronze and the other the Siamese gun inlaid with silver that had been seized from the royal storehouse the day before. It was Louis XIV's toy, then, that would end the old regime in Paris." (Schama, 1980, 313). Regardless, the rebels had to make do with whatever arms they could obtain, and they also assumed they had a limited time to act since royalist cavalry and infantry were encamped nearby. The fear that these troops might march to the relief of the Bastille and butcher everyone in their path had to worry the besiegers.

The besiegers covered their preparations by rolling a wagon filled with burning straw forward, thereby concealing their guns from the Bastille's marksmen. This clever strategy enabled the revolutionary gunners to set up and load their cannons undisturbed by musket fire, and the flames streaming from the wagon also set fire to the governor's house, providing even more of a smoke screen and possibly serving to dishearten de Launay as well.

As soon as the ceremonial cannon was charged with powder and round shot, and a fuse applied to the touch-hole, the gun exploded rather than firing. Transformed into shrapnel, the pieces of the burst barrel mowed down the men standing near it. The besiegers soon brought up a new artillery piece, however, and a mortar which they had found, before opening fire on the walls. However, the cannonballs merely glanced off the 10 foot thick stone, knocking a few chips loose but creating no serious damage.

At this point, the besiegers moved their cannons to point at the third drawbridge. Lieutenant de la Flue and his 10 men beat a hasty retreat from the position they had held until then, standing in front of the drawbridge to deliver a point-blank volley if the mob returned. De la Flue recalled, "During this time I had withdrawn my men from in front of the gate, so as not to leave them exposed to the fire of the enemy, with which we were threatened." (Bingham, 1901, 280).

De Launay observed the rebel artillery being set up to aim at the final drawbridge and immediately decided to surrender if he could get good terms. De la Flue protested and urged that they should continue resisting, but de Launay ignored him, and at the governor's command, the defenders waved a handkerchief through one of the holes de la Flue had cut in the third drawbridge for his artillery pieces, using this signal in lieu of a white flag. Second Lieutenant Elie, the de facto leader of the second attack, advanced personally to take the letter held out through the improvised embrasure by de la Flue. In this missive, de Launay offered to surrender the Bastille if good terms were offered to him and his men. However, when the letter was read to them, the "Conquerors" raised a disdainful roar: "Down with the drawbridges! No capitulation!"

A strange incident occurred at this point, and it resulted in the only time during the day when the Bastille's defenders fired one of their artillery pieces. A young woman was seized by the crowd as she attempted to hide in the outer courtyard, and the multitude immediately came to the incorrect conclusion that she was the daughter of de Launay himself. She was carried in the second courtyard and was placed on a mattress, which the rioters then set on fire. They shouted to de Launay to have the gate opened or they would burn his daughter. The woman's true father, a minor prison official named de Monsigny, ran to the edge of the roof and was shot and killed by one of the revolutionaries in the courtyard below. One of the revolutionary citizens, a man named Aubin Bonnemere, was disgusted at the spectacle and shoved his way through the other rioters to lift the woman off the burning mattress. Though showered with insults and death threats, he successfully rescued her and escaped unharmed himself.

The garrison was also outraged at this sight and fired one of their cannons, the only piece of defending ordnance to be heard that day. The shot tore a bloody lane through the revolutionaries, killing several of them, but ironically, this was just about the last act of defiance on the part of the defenders. At this moment, four of the pensioners under de la Flue's command disobeyed orders and rushed forward to open the last drawbridge and admit the mob. The horde surged inside, taking the other pensioners and de la Flue prisoner and placing them under guard while the Bastille was ransacked. De Launay carried a torch into the cellars, meaning to set off the powder in a last calamitous act of revenge that would likely have killed everybody inside the fortress, but de Launay was grappled and dragged away from the powder at the last moment by two of the defending soldiers, Ferrand and Bequard. As fate would have it, Bequard was one of the few defenders killed by the victorious "Conquerors," who cut off his hands before hanging him from a lamppost. Those who killed him never realized they owed their lives to his actions.

As it turned out, de Launay's attempt to surrender probably saved the lives of most of his men, but it cost him his own life in gristly fashion and led to the eventual demolition of the medieval fortress. Nevertheless, at the moment of surrender, the Bastille's physical destruction was likely not even contemplated by those who had just taken it; after all, the powder was the main issue in the minds of the men who had just defeated the Bastille's garrison. The Gardes Francaises were disciplined and responsible professional soldiers, and they did their best to ensure that the prisoners went unharmed. This effort was mostly successful, and the majority of the pensioners either joined the revolutionaries immediately or were simply disarmed and released. Only one man had been killed on the defending side during the Storming of the Bastille, but the attackers had suffered some 98 deaths, somewhere between 10%-15% of their total force.

Most of the Swiss soldiers also escaped unscathed. They had thrown off their heavy uniform coats to be better able to fire through loopholes in the cramped spaces of the Bastille, and now they wore only their linen waistcoats and breeches. Remarkably, the rioters thought this was some kind of prison uniform and that the Swiss were political prisoners of the Bourbons, so they simply permitted them to leave. Many eventually found their way back to their encamped regiment.

De Launay and de la Flue were not so lucky. To their credit, Second Lieutenant Elie and Pierre-Augustin Hulin attempted to escort de Launay, unharmed, to the Hotel de Ville, where the Revolutionary Committee could decide his fate. However, there was only so much they could do. De Launay was knocked down and beaten savagely several times on the way, and the two self-appointed officers attempted to prevent his assassination at this point.

A painting depicting the seizure of de Launay

When de Launay arrived at the Hotel de Ville, the mob realized they were about to be cheated of their prey and closed in. A debate began about what method of killing de Launay would be most painful, and one suggestion was to drag him to death over the cobblestones while tied behind a horse. The governor, dreading a lingering death, roared, "Let me die!" Showing a frantic burst of energy, he kicked a nearby pastry cook named Duliat or Desnot squarely in the genitals with his heavy riding boots. In response, the crowd lunged forward, piercing his body with knives, bayonets, and swords. De Launay toppled into the gutter, still alive but horribly wounded. Finally, some of the men nearby discharged their pistols into his writhing body, and a butcher named Mathieu Jouve Jourdan attacked his neck with a saw, finally decapitating him.

Three of the pensioners were hanged by the mob, but Louis de la Flue had a narrow escape which he himself recounted: "It was with this look-out that I entered the Hotel de Ville. I was presented to a committee which was sitting there. I was accused of being one of the defenders of the Bastille and of having caused blood to flow. I justified myself as well as I could, saying that I had to obey orders. Not seeing any other means of escaping execution, with the remainder of my men, I declared that I wished to serve the city and the nation. I do not know if they were tired of slaying, or if my reasons convinced them, but they were applauded, and there was a general cry raised of 'Bravo! bravo, gallant Swiss!' In an instant wine was brought, and I had to drink to the city and the nation." (Bingham, 1901, 283-284). The resourceful lieutenant eventually made his way back to the Salis-Samade regiment, where he filed his report and disappeared from history.

The 20,000 pounds of powder was the true objective of those storming the Bastille, but, carried away as they were by revolutionary fervor, they also freed the prisoners they found. Of course, after listening to and spreading their own propaganda, the mob was rather surprised to find just seven inmates in the whole edifice. Four of these men were forgers who took the opportunity to vanish into the crowd, while two were patently insane and were soon committed to asylums elsewhere in the country. The other prisoner was a debauched noble who had been temporarily locked up at his family's request.

Nevertheless, these seven were paraded and feted as martyrs of liberty released from tyranny's dungeon, and a bizarre farce followed. The "Conquerors" were somewhat baffled at the total lack of torture instruments in the reformed late-18th century prison, so they brought out a few pieces of rusted armor from the Middle Ages and some parts from the prison printing press and displayed these as pieces of "torture machines." This ludicrous falsehood actually managed to evoke a response from the crowd.

The Bastille itself was quickly demolished. An intelligent and predatory entrepreneur, Pierre-Francois Palloy, was on the site the next day, the 15th of July, with 800 workmen to begin demolition. Though this had not yet been decided upon by the Committee, the go-ahead was soon received, and Palloy's men leveled the fortress in a few weeks time. Not only was Palloy paid handsomely for the demolition, he also salvaged the materials necessary to create and sell tens of thousands of souvenirs, including scale models of the Bastille, which were immensely popular. Palloy, at least, turned a huge profit from the Storming of the Bastille.

The Fall of King Louis XVI

Significant political changes came in the weeks following the storming of the Bastille, as the National Assembly responded to the rioting and violence with legal changes. First, the Assembly encouraged people to remain calm, continue paying their taxes, and be patient while the Assembly created a new legal structure. On August 4, a motion was made to abolish feudalism.

The original motion was fairly simple, but it was soon expanded far beyond its intentions. It took more than a week to draft a formal decree of the decisions made during the National Assembly meeting of August 4. The final motion destroyed more than just the institution of feudalism. It also destroyed the very notion of privilege for the nobility and clergy, brought a formal end to the selling of offices, and defined social classes. While the motion was more extensive than intended, it did succeed in calming the violence across the countryside.

The National Assembly, which had renamed itself the National Constituent Assembly on July 7, had begun work on a new constitution on July 9. Robespierre was widely admired during the constitutional discussions for his calm manner. He supported freedom of religion and freedom of the press during constitutional discussions, as well as distinct and separate legislative and executive branches of government. While he added to the discussions and debates, he did not distinguish himself.

Work continued through August 4, beginning again after the extensive discussions on the night of August 4. On August 26, 1789, the National Assembly voted on the Declaration of the Rights of Man and the Citizen. While they retained the right to alter or change the Declaration of the Rights of Man, it would become the foundation of the French Revolution and one of the hallmark documents of universal human rights. The Declaration of the Rights of Man consists of 17 articles, defending the right of law, property rights, equal taxation and supporting the notion that power rests in the people, not the King. As in the Constitution of the United States of America, the rights to freedom of religion and speech are protected in the Declaration of Rights.

Mirabeau and others, called monarchiens, pushed for a constitutional monarchy, consisting of a King with veto power and two legislative bodies. One of those bodies, like the House of Commons in Great Britain, was an elected body, while the other would be an inherited body, like the House of Lords. The National Assembly voted down the monarchist proposal for an inherited body by a significant majority, but the veto decision was more complex. Only a small minority in the National Assembly wanted to deny the King any sort of veto rights. Many supported a limited veto power, and Necker indicated the King might accede to this. As the King had still not given his approval to the August measures, there was some desire for a solution that would meet everyone's needs in early September. A suspensive veto passed, without public support, on September 15.

When the National Assembly created a committee to draft a new constitution, radical publisher Jean-Paul Marat sent more than 20 documents directly to the Assembly, but he received no response. And when the Assembly issued the Declaration of the Rights of Man and the Citizen on August 28, it affirmed the right to private property, in opposition to Marat's views on natural rights. Still, and probably more importantly, the Declaration also provided for the right to free speech, critical for Marat's future work.

Marat

A month later, Marat printed the first issue of his daily newspaper, first called the Publiciste Parisien. It was renamed only four days later, on September 16, the Ami du Peuple, or "The Friend of the People". From the beginning, the Friend of the People became a fictional character, embodying the revolutionary patriot, and when Marat addressed his readers in these early issues, he signed himself, "Marat, editeur d'Ami du Peuple". Eventually, he changed his signature to read simply, "Marat, Ami du Peuple", thereby naming himself the friend of the people. The people, in this instance, were the workers who had stormed the Bastille. Called the sans-culottes, the workers of Paris wore long pants, rather than the knee pants and stockings of the aristocracy. They were craftsmen, tradesmen, skilled workers and shopkeepers.

The Ami du Peuple was a daily newspaper. Each day's printing costs were approximately the equivalent of one month's wages for an unskilled worker in the city. He printed approximately 2,000 copies per day in the first months after the debut of his paper; however, the actual distribution was much higher. Each copy was read by multiple people and newspapers like Marat's were often read aloud. Eventually, circulation reached as much as 6,000 copies each day. Printing still required hand presses and was a labor-intensive process. Even with multiple presses and employees, large print runs were a challenge.

Marat had a significant network of friends and allies who enabled him to maintain his work during periods when he could not work openly. Many citizens offered him shelter in their homes, as he slept in various places to avoid detection. The distributors of the Ami du Peuple risked arrest each day as they sold copies. Multiple intermediaries helped to protect Marat, acting as go-betweens between the editor and various printshops.

Grain prices, which had fallen slightly, rose again in September, leading tiots and violence in the streets to resume across France. The situation was, to contemporaries, much like the one that sparked the storming of the Bastille in July. On the 14th of September, Louis XVI called the disciplined and faithful Flanders Regiment to Versailles. With the support of this military force, the King's confidence grew, and he finally responded to the motions set forth by the National Assembly in August. Rather than offering his support, he agreed to publish, but not promulgate the decree of August 11. On October 4, Louis XVI expressed serious reservations about the Declaration of Rights.

By September 1789, Marat was no longer a reformist supporting the notion of a constitutional monarchy. He began to question both the Paris Commune and National Assembly, calling them enemies of a true revolution. The Assembly and Commune were largely made up of the wealthy, eliminating the access of the sans-culottes to the new political establishment. There were many political journals, newspapers and daily papers in Paris; however, Ami du Peuple soon distinguished itself as one of the most radical.

Regardless of laws supporting the free press, Marat was summoned before the city council on September 25, 1789. He had criticized the Subsistence Committee, calling it a part of the food shortage problem rather than a solution. While Marat waited for several days for his meeting before the city council, when he finally spoke, he was not charged and was simply allowed to leave and continue publishing. His criticisms of the Subsistence Committee, while disliked, were not dishonest.

While Marat had not been involved in the storming of the Bastille, he played a significant role in the October Days that led to the royal family's removal from Versailles. In early October, Marat reported on a "counterrevolutionary orgy" at the Palace of Versailles. Accusations included the trampling of the cockade, the red and blue symbol of the Revolution and open insults to the Revolution. According to Marat's confidential source, members of the Royal Army and National Guard were present. It was even suggested that the Queen had sexual relations with members of the Army and Guard. While there was some truth to the accusations of disrespect for the cockade during a drunken party, many of Marat's statements were nothing more than rumor.

A reception on October 1 to welcome the Flanders Regiment caused a number of rumors to spread through Paris. Many present became quite drunk, expressed anti-patriotic sentiments and trampled the cockade. Those present at the banquet feasted, while bread shortages were rampant elsewhere. While the reception was, undoubtedly, a poor choice given the political situation, the rumors were far worse than the reality. Accusations of an orgy involving the Queen were common throughout Paris.

Marat did not just report on the incident, but encouraged the people of Paris to march on Versailles and force the King and royal family to come to Paris. The call to insurrection was published on the morning of October 5, and as fate would have it market women began a march toward Versailles on that very morning.

As the National Assembly kept working toward writing a new constitution, market women began a march toward Versailles on the morning of October 5, 1789. The market women, traditionally allowed some access to the Queen, had several demands. They intended to demand grain or flour in the face of shortages and high food costs, as well as forcing the King to accede to certain aspects of the constitution that would reduce royal power. When the mob reached Versailles, Robespierre met them. He sympathized with their concerns, agreeing at once that the food shortages were the result of intentional actions and ordering an inquiry. While he did not change the course of events on that October day or those that followed, he did preserve the role of the National Assembly as a friend of the people, including the poor.

Engraving of the Women's March on Versailles

The royal family began their day quite normally. The Queen was at the Petit Trianon with friends while the King hunted. But word came that afternoon that the mob was on its way, and while some in the court wanted the Queen and children to leave for a more secure palace twelve miles away, she refused.

A single woman was allowed to speak to the King, pleading their cause. He agreed to order the release of two stores of grains, providing that order in writing. The King, growing concerned by the situation, also agreed to sign preliminary agreements regarding the constitution. However, by that evening, thousands were gathered outside the palace, and the mob no longer consisted just of market women. Armed brigands had joined the mob, along with a number of other men and women.

Although thousands of National Guardsmen under the orders of the Marquis de Lafayette were positioned ostensibly to defend the Royal Family, early in the morning of October 6, the gathered mob stormed the Queen's bedroom, but she escaped to the King's chamber, via a secret staircase that had been constructed to facilitate marital relations between the young couple. Their goal was a direct attack on the Queen, and though she escaped, two of her bodyguards were killed in the assault. Forced to leave the Palace, the royal family was accompanied not only by those gathered outside Versaille, but by the heads of those killed in the attack on the Palace, born aloft on spikes. The mob forced the King, Queen, and their children to move into an unused palace in Paris, the Tuileries. A procession of more than 60,000 accompanied the King, most unfriendly. The National Assembly followed the King to Paris a few days later. Many of the remaining nobles at Versailles left the Palace, seeking refuge outside of France. The National Assembly followed, taking up new quarters in Paris, after it closed the session on October 15.

Following his meeting with the market women on October 5, Robespierre found his voice in the National Assembly. His name now appeared in the press with some frequency, and he became a well-known personality in the Assembly, though he suffered failures in addition to successes. While he argued passionately for issues that mattered to him, including the elimination of the lettres de cachet and rights of the poor to vote and serve in the National Guard, he was ridiculed when he suggested a new format to publish the laws of the Assembly. Later, he was frustrated by his inability to make a prepared speech before the delegates.

Constitutional arguments were not the only subjects discussed at the National Assembly. The Assembly also dealt with the organization and structure of Paris and the role of the Church. Robespierre's speeches on the organization of the city were not well-received, even by his allies in the Assembly. He believed that the Church served a valuable function, but he wished to make Church offices elected and even allow priests to marry. This suggestion was so at odds with religious dogma and so scandalous that such conversation was put to an immediate end.

Somewhat surprisingly, even during this tumultuous time, life continued in many normal ways in Paris. There were concerts and plays, people walking in the parks and homes and stables to lease. Music teachers, optometrists, hairdressers and pharmacists offered services in the city, while theaters and opera houses offered plays and performances with a revolutionary spirit. Luxury goods, including food and clothing, were still available in the city, at least for those with the funds to pay for them. While there were incidents of revolutionary violence, they were relatively few and did not impact many in the city.

Following the women's march to Versailles, the Paris Commune reacted to Marat's actions by ordering his arrest. Marat went underground, but he still managed to continue publishing Ami du

Peuple after a short break. It took approximately a month for him to resume publishing between October 8, when he went into hiding, and November 5, when the next issue appeared. By November, Marat had his own presses, but publication was erratic, and Marat was finally arrested and imprisoned briefly in December.

Despite this first arrest, all charges were dropped, but each time Marat had to deal with city officials, he published a full account of the event. Naturally, that didn't make him many friends, and in late January, after several weeks of unbroken publication, arrest warrants were again issued for Marat.

This time, however, Marat now had the protection of other journalists and of his local district where the Ami du Peuple was based, the Cordeliers district. The Cordeliers district argued the legality of the arrest warrants. A young lawyer in the Cordeliers, Georges Jacques Danton came to Marat's defense. Marat's power over the people of Paris became clear when the mayor of Paris, Bailly, called in the National Guard to raid Marat's printshop and offices. Danton threatened to sound the tocsin, the bells calling the people to rise up in insurrection, warning that everyone in the district, including the women, was armed and prepared to fight for Marat. There was a long standoff, but Marat escaped with the help of the Cordeliers district.

Georges Jacques Danton

After that close call, Marat decided to go into exile in England, but he continued to publish revolutionary pamphlets, including the "Appeal to the Nation," which told the story of his own revolutionary struggles. In the "Appeal to the Nation," Marat called for a dictator to move the revolution to its end, and he also called for the execution of those who were to blame for the poverty of the people. While his support for a dictator seems idiosyncratic at best and hypocritical at worst, Marat envisioned this as a temporary rather than permanent situation. He was, however, certain that violence was a necessity in the Revolution, writing in his paper that year, "Five or six hundred heads would have guaranteed your freedom and happiness but a false humanity has restrained your arms and stopped your blows. If you don't strike now, millions of your brothers will die, your enemies will triumph and your blood will flood the streets. They'll slit your throats without mercy and disembowel your wives. And their bloody hands will rip out your children's entrails to erase your love of liberty forever."

After being forcibly marched to the Tuileries, Louis XVI was no longer King of France. His new title was King of the French, indicating that his power came solely from the people of France. Even so, he now had little political power. His suspensive veto allowed him to postpone legislation, but nothing more, and though he still chose ministers, they could be impeached by the National Assembly. His ministers could not be chosen from the legislature. In addition to limits on the King's authority, the legislature set out regulations for its own election and governance, as well as electoral policies for civic offices.

While the royal family had not used the Tuileries in some time, it was inhabited by a large number of royal servants and their families. Built in the 16th century, the Palace was in considerable disrepair. Over the coming months, the family had furnishings brought from Versailles and continued daily life, much as it had been in Versailles. The Queen continued to order new dresses from her favorite dressmaker, Rose Bertin, and the family was granted a generous allowance by the National Assembly and had revenues from their own estates. The Comte and Comtesse de Provence and the King's sister, Elisabeth, were also forced to leave Versailles, and the two living aunts also took up residence in the Tuileries. The Comte and Comtesse de Provence retired to their own palace.

The family continued to gather for diplomatic affairs and regular family dinners, but the King's depression worsened and he took no actions on their behalf, even as the Queen sent messengers throughout Europe requesting aid. The Queen continued many of her own duties and hobbies, from charity work to playing billiards with the King. The family was guarded by members of the National Guard, but they were allowed a great deal of freedom during the first summer of their confinement. Still, they took no action to escape.

The Revolution moved quickly and soon it was the first anniversary of the storming of the Bastille Day. Plans were delayed and the final decisions made with only a few weeks to prepare. People from all over the city came out to help prepare the Champ de Mars for a parade of the National Guard, witnessed by the Assembly and the King. The National Guard, under the leadership of Lafayette, would pass beneath a triumphant arch and make a vow of loyalty and patriotism at an altar to the fatherland. In the grand pavilion, Robespierre stood very near to the King himself, as an equal. After the Guard swore an oath, the King was asked to swear an oath to act on the decisions of the Assembly. Many, but not Robespierre, still believed in the possibility of a constitutional monarchy in July 1790.

The Festival of Federation came just as the changing French government faced the possibility of war with Austria. The press denounced the Festival of Federation, including Desmoulins. Desmoulins and even more radical members of the press, like Jean-Paul Marat, were broadly criticized in the Assembly. The Assembly began to restrict the freedom of the press and brought charges against a number of figures, including Desmoulins. Desmoulins escaped punishment with the help of Robespierre.

On July 31, 1790, the National Assembly ordered the arrest of all "authors, printers and distributors who incite the people to insurrection". While Robespierre came to Desmoulins' defense, no one spoke for Marat, and the indictment was altered to apply only to Marat. Desmoulins had a long history with the Revolution and was a school friend of Robespierre's.

Publication of the Ami du Peuple continued, but Marat himself remained fully in hiding. By August 1790, from the basements where he hid and wrote, Marat called for a purging of the officers of the National Guard, the deaths of 800 members of the National Assembly and the burning of the remaining ministers of the state. Marat's words at this time reflected the division between the Assembly, monarchists, National Guard and more radical elements, including the Jacobins, the Cordeliers, and Robespierre. Marat was starting to accumulate growing support from the Jacobins, who called for him to be able to publish freely.

In April 1791, the President of the National Assembly, the Comte de Mirabeau died, likely of advanced stages of syphilis. While Mirabeau and Robespierre had never been close, Robespierre had a sort of grudging admiration for Mirabeau, even if he did not exemplify the ideals of morality and virtue.

Mirabeau's death brought an end to the hope for a peaceful solution with a constitutional monarchy. Robespierre argued for Mirabeau's right to a patriotic burial and his ashes were interred in the newly-completed Church of Saint-Genevieve, now called the Pantheon. However, during the King's trial nearly 2 years later, Mirabeau's work as an intercessor between the monarchy and Assembly was discovered, and he was disgraced; his remains were removed from the Pantheon and re-buried anonymously. The Assembly was now much more divided, with radical factions, including the Jacobins, rapidly gaining power.

Marat had been one of the few to speak out against Mirabeau shortly after his death, accusing him accurately as it turned out. "Riquetti [Mirabeau] is no more; he dies victim of his numerous treasons, victim of his too tardy scruples, victim of the barbarous foresight of his atrocious accomplices. Adroit rogues who are to be found in all circles have sought to play upon your pity, and already duped by their false discourse, you mourn this traitor as the most zealous of your defenders; they have represented his death as a public calamity, and you bewail him as a hero, as the savior of your country, who has sacrificed himself for you."

Throughout 1791, Robespierre continued to speak out strongly against capital punishment. He believed the death penalty was unfair and moreover, an ineffective deterrent. Individuals only had the right to kill in self-defense, so Robespierre believed the same rule sould apply to the state. But while Robespierre disagreed with the death penalty at all costs at this stage of his career, others in the Assembly were merely seeking a more humane solution to capital punishment. Executions varied prior to the Revolution. The nobility were typically beheaded, but this was not always a fast process. The poor were most commonly hung. Depending upon the crime, a more severe punishment and slower death might be ordered. A committee had developed a new machine, making a clean, swift death more accessible. A sharp blade severed the head, eliminating the risk of human error in the execution process. On June 3, 1791, the Assembly voted to retain the death penalty, but all, regardless of crime or wealth, would be beheaded with the new machine, called the guillotine.

Over the course of the fall and winter of 1790, the situation for the royal family worsened. Political intrigues continued, with some, including the Princess Elisabeth, calling for civil war. Conflict within the Church added to the challenges. Publications on the Revolution ranged from serious texts to, not surprisingly, vulgar pamphlets. The aunts left the Tuileries in February 1791, causing a great deal of controversy. Discussions of escape increased, particularly as the state took a greater interest in the Dauphin.

In June 1791, the royal family attempted to escape, with the assistance of Count Axel von Fersen. Preparations had began in December 1790, when the berlin, or large carriage, was ordered. The berlin would include cooking facilities, a toiletry case, chamber pots and other essentials, making it a relatively luxurious means of transit. On the night of June 20, 1791, the royal family fled the Tuileries disguised as servants, while the servants disguised as nobles. When the King fled the Tuileries, he left behind a long proclamation. No longer did he feign any support for the revolution or a constitutional monarchy. The document he left at the Tuileries clearly denounced the actions of the National Assembly.

The King had also refused to take along any other experienced soldiers, perhaps condemning their escape to failure. Travelling in a large single carriage, the King was recognized approximately 160 miles from Paris at Varennes, and the National Guard returned the family to the Tuileries. The royal family was met with near silence by crowds as their carriage returned.

While the royal family attempted to make its escape across France, Robespierre worked to maintain his close social network. He spent June 20, the second anniversary of the tennis court oath, in Versailles with the Jacobin club. When he returned to Paris, he learned of the King's arrest. Bailly, fully aware of the truth of the situation, put forth the story that the King and royal family had been kidnapped and taken against their will. The Assembly, acting on June 22nd to preserve the peace, declared that the King had been kidnapped and suggested that his denunciations were made under duress. While the National Assembly covered for the King, creating a fiction, he now had no power at all. Political clubs, including the Jacobin clubs, began to call for the removal of the King. At the same time, a few Jacobin clubs began to call for the formation of a republic, rather than a constitutional monarchy.

Robespierre made his most radical speech to date at the Jacobin Club on the night after the King's escape. In his speech, he actively criticized the Assembly's choice to create a story about the King's escape. According to Robespierre, Louis XVI, the "prime public functionary" of France, had chosen to abandon the country at a critical juncture. The country had enemies, but he was not speaking of Austria or Prussia. According to Robespierre, "our enemies speak the same language as us". Robespierre was less concerned about Austria or Prussia than counter-revolutionary forces within France, disguised as patriots. The constitution was nearly complete and, as Robespierre saw it, had some significant issues. The King's escape attempt had not just discredited him, but also Lafayette and the Assembly.

Robespierre realized that he might, in fact, have gone too far. He prepared his will and feared for his life. While his life was not threatened by his words, they did split the Jacobins. A large number of Assembly deputies left the Jacobins, forming the Feuillants. The Feuillants remained committed to a constitutional monarchy. Prior to the King's escape, Robespierre was preparing for a quiet future as a public prosecutor in Paris. That future was fundamentally changed when he broke with the Assembly, declaring himself in opposition to the monarchy.

By July 14, 1791, the second anniversary of the storming of the Bastille, the celebration was much less grand. Only 24 deputies attended the small-scale festivities at the Champ de Mars, Robespierre among them. By now, nearly 18 months before it would actually take place, Robespierre had already begun to call for the trial of Louis XVI. In the days following the anniversary, the Assembly announced that the King had been suspended, bringing an end to the Jacobin petition for the King's trial. While the Jacobins withdrew their petition, the Club of the Cordeliers did not. Led by a friend of Robespierre's, Georges Jacques Danton, petitioners gathered at the Champ de Mars on July 17. National guardsmen, under the command of Lafayette, attempted to suppress the petitioners, opening fire. Approximately 50 petitioners were killed that day, and Lafayette declared martial law. Robespierre wept for the patriots killed at the Champ de Mars at the Jacobin club that night, and when some National Guardsmen approached the Jacobins, Robespierre again feared for his life.

At the end of July, Louis XVI himself began to call for peace under the constitution and officially requested the Comte d'Artois stop any efforts at rebellion and return. Laws in August restricted the freedom of the press in an attempt to avoid additional violence, and by early fall, the constitution was complete. While the constitution included some provisions with respect to the King, it included none for the by now hated Queen. On September 13, 1791, Louis XVI signed the constitution, largely as it had been first conceived in 1789. The King now acted solely on the orders of the Assembly, and the following April, under the orders of the Legislative Assembly, the King declared war on Austria. That only made the Marie Antoinette's position more tenuous, and distaste for the royal family, particularly the Austrian Queen, continued, with a mob calling for her death in June 1792.

The Formation of the Republic

During the late spring of 1792, Brissot and his circle of close acquaintances began to call for the formation of a French Republic. Robespierre opposed the very notion of a republic, less because of any political sentiment and more because of his personal objections to Brissot. Robespierre now argued strongly against his former friend, going so far as to blame Brissot for the massacre on the Champs de Mars a year earlier. For the first time, Robespierre even began to argue for the existence of a constitutional monarchy, a position at odds with what he had been advocating for years. But even while Robespierre went in this new direction and distanced himself from Brissot and Madame Roland after his return from Arras, her salon became a center for discussions of a republican future for France.

While Robespierre argued in favor of a constitutional monarchy, the King's legislative veto powers were about to be tried. The Assembly had already ordered any priest who refused to submit to the state banished and deported, bringing it to great odds with the Catholic Church. Clergy became state employees, elected by their parish, and now the Assembly wanted the clergy to be required to make an oath of loyalty to the state. According to Church law, clergy could not swear an oath without papal approval. The Pope considered the oath required of the clergy for some time, finally issuing an answer in April 1791 denouncing the new French constitution. Priests who took the oath, called jurors, were excommunicated from the Church. (Later, priests who complied with the Church, called non-juring priests, were punished for their actions and were, eventually, sentenced to death in 1793.)

Fearing the King would veto the Assembly's initiative, a large protest was planned for the third anniversary of the tennis court oath. The protestors were eventually allowed into the gardens of the Tuileries, frightening the royal family. Petion broke up the demonstration, but Lafayette returned to Paris from the French border and called for the punishment of the demonstrators and an end to the Jacobins. The threat to the Jacobins from Lafayette brought the distinct factions, including Brissot's and Robespierre's, together, now uniting them against a single enemy. In response to Lafayette, Robespierre viciously and publicly attacked him, "General, while from the midst of your camp you declared war upon me, which you had thus far spared for the enemies of our state, while you denounced me as an enemy of liberty to the army, national guard and Nation in letters published by your purchased papers, I had thought myself only disputing with a general... but not yet the dictator of France, arbitrator of the state."

Throughout late July, the call for an official end to the monarchy began to cross class lines. The Jacobins expressed growing support for an insurrection, with Robespierre calling for an insurrection on July 29. The patriots of the Revolution feared the incursion of Austrian and Prussian forces that would support the right of the King to rule and bring an end to the

Revolution, so on July 28, the Assembly opened access to the National Guard to all, regardless of financial status. Gradually, sections of the city government began to add their voices to the demand for the deposition of the King.

One group in the Assembly had hoped for discontent while still favoring the monarchy. Brissot and his allies, called Girondins, had expected that the King would restore them to power. Initially, many of the Girondins belonged to the Jacobins, and some, like Brissot, had been friends of the more radical elemenst, including Marat and Robespierre, in the past.

In August, anti-monarchial forces began to act in earnest. Danton formed the Insurrectionary Commune on August 9 and took over the city of Paris, and the insurrectionists prepared to attack the Tuileries, where the royal family was still staying. The Tuileries were heavily guarded, and the loss of life was expected to be high.

In June 1792, a mob had appeared at the Tuileries, calling for the death of the Queen. While the mob was broken up, the incident was repeated on August 9, 1792. On the night of August 10, 1792, a mob stormed the Tuileries and forced the royal family to flee and beg the Assembly for safety and protection. A massacre followed the King's departure, perhaps as the result of his failure to order a cease-fire as they fled, and the revolutionaries or sans-culottes killed many within the palace. More than 1,000 people died in the attack on the Tuileries, but with the royal family forced to flee, it was widely considered a victory. And in the wake of the attacks that night, the French monarchy was officially dissolved in September 1792.

Depiction of members of the Paris Commune storming the Tuileries Palace and massacring the Swiss Guards

The royal family escaped to the National Assembly hall, a converted riding school, nearby. While they hoped for safety and sanctuary, they were moved into new, more prison-like accommodations, and the King was officially suspended. Lafayette fled France for his life.

The royal family spent that first night in a few rooms in a nearby sixteenth-century convent. As a response, the Assembly, listening to the wishes of the Paris Commune, had the family imprisoned in a medieval complex, known as the Tower. The Tower consisted of the Great Tower, a rather run-down palace and the Small Tower, a prison-like building. It was a far cry from Versailles; the rooms were poor and infested with vermin, and the walls in Marie-Therese's chamber were decorated with pornographic engravings, which the King himself removed. The family was still permitted to live together and was relatively well-treated, but allowed only a few attendants, including the Princesse de Lamballe. They did have access to books, needlework, and even a small dog. Even at this late date, receipts reveal the family received generous meals, as well as some clothing purchases during their imprisonment. They were told their accommodations were temporary and that new rooms were being prepared in the new Tower. A few attendants, including the Queen's longtime friend, the Princesse de Lamballe were housed alongside the royal family between August 10 and August 19.

Robespierre served in his local section of Paris, called the section of pikes, prior to his election to the Insurrectionary Commune, the governing body now in control of Paris. Only days after the protest, Petion requested a return to the municipal government, but the Commune did not back down once it acquired power. The division between Petion and Robespierre would never be reconciled. On August 16, Robespierre presented a petition from the Commune to the Legislative Assembly demanding that a revolutionary tribunal be established and a new national convention be convened and voted upon by universal suffrage.

While the royal family had been allowed a few attendants when they took up residence in the Tower on August 10, by August 19, the Commune began interrogating and trying royalists for a variety of crimes against the state. The royal attendants were taken to the prison of La Force, and on September 2, 1792, Louis and Marie Antoinette could hear cannons throughout the city. The prisons were being attacked and many of the royalist prisoners, not only in Paris, but also Versailles and Rheims, were massacred. Mobs entered the prisons and massacred prisoners, many of whom were royalists or non-compliant priests. The Queen's close friend, the Princesse de Lamballe, was simply thrown to the mob after a mock trial by a makeshift tribunal and murdered, with her head placed on a pike and marched around. Between 1,100 and 1,400 people were killed between September 2 and September 7, and the Commune did not act to stop the September massacres, either due to inability to stop the violence or a fundamental belief that the people were in the right.

At Robespierre's insistence, the Commune created a tribunal to investigate counter-revolutionary activities. During its first four months, between August and December 1792, the committee sentenced 28 people to die by the guillotine. Most of those sentenced were ordinary criminals, rather than political prisoners.

The Duke of Brunswick marched toward Paris with a trained army to defend the King. When French forces, consisting of a combination of trained soldiers, National Guard troops and volunteers, met the Duke of Brunswick's army, they were successful. The forces of Europe did not successfully stop the Revolution and change had become an unstoppable force. The makeshift French army even went on the offensive, succeeding in the Austrian Netherlands and declaring war on England and the Dutch Republic. War losses would eventually lead to a conscription policy, requisitioning new troops from throughout the country.

The change in administration enabled Marat to come out of hiding, and he announced his return from hiding with a public placard and called for the trial of the King, arming patriots, and the execution of counterrevolutionaries. Marat took a seat on the Commune's leading council, the Committee of Surveillance, and for its part the Paris Commune showed its support of Marat and his colleagues by providing them with confiscated presses. Marat and Simone Evrard moved into a new home and workplace, and on August 13, the Ami du Peuple announced its support for the new government.

However, Marat's support was short-lived, and soon he began to express serious fears of counterrevolutionaries in the government, fears shared by Robespierre and many others in the government. The two men respected one another throughout their respective careers, but they met in person only once. The Council created a tribunal to try anyone accused of a political crime on August 17, and the first political prisoner was executed on August 21. Travel outside the city became increasingly difficult; a passport was required, along with a certificate de civisme, issued by sectional Committees of Surveillance.

Faced with a growing military threat, Danton called for the sans-culottes to step up and fight for the Revolution, fighting against an external enemy, rather than an internal one. While there were many volunteers, there were significant concerns about the imprisoned counterrevolutionaries who would remain in the city, since there had been approximately 3,000 political arrests in the days following the August 10 insurrection. On September 2, the sans-culottes, without the support of Marat or others in the administration, broke into the prisons and began to slaughter prisoners, both common criminals and counterrevolutionaries. Tribunals spared some of the prisoners, but not others; former Queen Marie Antoinette's close friend, the Princesse de Lamballe, was among those killed in the September massacres.

While Marat did not condemn the actions, he did express regret for the criminals killed, considering it an unfortunate excess. He certainly supported the execution of counterrevolutionaries, however, and he personally was more concerned with the National Convention elections, taking place that same month. Among the Jacobins, Robespierre and his followers accused Brissot and the Girondins, while the Girondins blamed Robespierre. The massacres of September 2 did calm the worries of the people and thousands of working men left Paris for the frontlines of the war willingly.

Elections began at once to choose representatives for a new constitutional assembly to create a constitution for the French Republic, and that September Robespierre, Danton and Desmoulins were all elected in Paris. Robespierre's younger brother, Augustin, served with the delegates from Arras. Marat and several of those he endorsed were elected to serve in the National Convention, and Marat's own election was likely secured by Robespierre's support. Painter Jacques-Louis David joined the Paris delegation, and Brissot was elected to serve by his hometown. Robespierre was a first deputy, but Petion was elected president of the first Convention, much to Robespierre's displeasure.

Petion, Brissot and their political allies became known as the Girondons. On September 20, 1792, trumpets announced the Republic of France. Marat continued to publish his newspaper, but following the declaration of the Republic, Marat renamed the Ami du Peuple. His publication was now Le Journal de la Republique Francaise. For the first time, Marat was working for the government, rather than against it. Marat voted with the left wing of the Convention, called the Mountain, which consisted of 24 deputies from Paris, along with the support of approximately 50 additional deputies; however, Marat considered himself to march alongside the Mountain rather than join with it.

Between the end of October and early November 1792, tensions between Robespierre and his allies and the Girondists rose substantially. The National Convention's first action, on the same day as the decisive Battle of Valmy which secured a French victory, was the declaration of a new French Republic. A year later, the new calendar of the French Republic would rely upon September 22, 1792 as the first day of Year One of the French Republic.

The Mountain was opposed by the Girondins, and from September to November 1792, tensions rose between the Jacobins and the Girondists. On September 25, the Girondins attacked Marat directly during speeches at the Convention, accusing him of conspiring with Robespierre and Danton to create a dictatorship. In response, Danton sought compromise with the Girondins and limited his support of Marat, and while Robespierre did not come to Marat's defense, he also did not attempt to distance himself.

Marat, upon finally being allowed to speak, acknowledged that he had many enemies in the Convention. The response from the Convention delegates was quite loud as they chanted "all of us". He informed the Convention that both Robespierre and Danton had denounced the notion of a dictatorship, regardless of his own belief in the necessity of it. The Girondins pulled out the final edition of the Ami du Peuple, calling for insurrection against the Convention, to which Marat responded with a more recent copy of his publication. The Convention voted on his arrest that day and refused to indict him, possibly because the upper galleries of their meeting hall were filled with Parisian sans-culottes. Marat's ability to speak and his ability to remain cool and collected served him well.

Members of the Girondons also condemned Robespierre, blaming him for the September massacres, and some Girondists, led by Marc-David Lasource, accused Robespierre of plotting to form a dictatorship. Girondist rumors insisted Robespierre, Marat and Danton all intended to create a triumvirate among them. Robespierre responded, "Upon the Jacobins I exercise, if we are to believe my accusers, a despotism of opinion, which can be regarded as nothing other than the forerunner of dictatorship. Firstly, I do not know what a dictatorship of opinion is, above all in a society of free men... unless this describes nothing more than the natural compulsion of principles. In fact, this compulsion hardly belongs to the man who enunciates them; it belongs to universal reason and to all men who wish to listen to its voice… Experience has proven, despite Louis XVI and his allies, that the opinion of the Jacobins and of the popular clubs were those of the French Nation; no citizen has made them, and I did nothing other than share in them."

Having equated the goals of the Jacobins with the people, Robespierre in turn accused the Girondists of seeking power and squelching the revolutionaries, firing back, "I will not remind you that the sole object of contention dividing us is that you have instinctively defended all acts of new ministers, and we, of principles; that you seemed to prefer power, and we equality... Why don't you prosecute the Commune, the Legislative Assembly, the Sections of Paris, the Assemblies of the Cantons and all who imitated us? For all these things have been illegal, as illegal as the Revolution, as the fall of the Monarchy and of the Bastille, as illegal as liberty itself... Citizens, do you want a revolution without a revolution? What is this spirit of persecution which has directed itself against those who freed us from chains?"

For the first time in these arguments, Robespierre also began to show that he believed that the ends justified the means. Extreme violence, even when it impacted the innocent, could be acceptable to the Revolution. In late October, Robespierre had the Girondists removed from the Jacobins.

Marat continued to take an active political role in the weeks that followed, and in his print work, he encouraged the sans-culottes to remain calm and avoid insurrection. When sans-culottes soldiers were accused of misconduct by Dumouriez, he defended them, both in the press and in the Convention. He predicted that Dumouriez would defect, but Dumouriez remained in control of a large military force for quite some time. Meanwhile, the Girondins continued to attack Marat at the Convention, and the Mountain did not offer support until the right wing faction gained military backing. Finally, Robespierre and the Mountain opted to support Marat.

With the French monarchy having officially been dissolved in September 1792, former King Louis XVI was now simply Louis Capet. The National Convention did not initially deal with what to do with the deposed King, but discussions as to his fate began at once. There were several options available, both with regards to trial and punishment. Some more radical members suggested that the people had already tried the King and found him guilty, and there were concerns that holding a trial might weaken the revolution. As far as punishments, imprisonment, banishment and execution were all considered. The United States, no doubt grateful for the former king's role in supporting the American Revolution, even offered the King and his family asylum.

In early October, the King was moved from the Tower where he shared rooms with his family to the Great Tower alone. The family was still allowed to eat together, but access to a number of items was restricted. The Queen and children moved into rooms in the Great Tower at the end of the month, which were nicely furnished and freshly decorated, but the respite in the Great Tower was short.

The Convention began to debate the trial of the King on November 13, 1792. A few voices opposed a trial, on the grounds that the constitution drafted by the National Assembly declared the person of the King inviolable. In response to that, Robespierre argued that Louis himself had violated the Constitution, so a Constitution declaring his inviolability could not now be used to save him. While Robespierre wanted the King punished, he did not support a trial. Instead, Robespierre and the up-and-coming Saint-Just supported an immediate execution, as the will of the people and the Revolution demanded. Before the trial, Robespierre wrote one of his most famous writings in support of the former king's death and against holding a trial:

Louis was a king, and our republic is established; the critical question concerning you must be decided by these words alone. Louis was dethroned by his crimes; Louis denounced the French people as rebels; he appealed to chains, to the armies of tyrants who are his brothers; the victory of the people established that Louis alone was a rebel; Louis cannot therefore be judged; he already is judged. He is condemned, or the republic cannot be absolved. To propose to have a trial of Louis XVI, in whatever manner one may, is to retrogress to royal despotism and constitutionality; it is a counter-revolutionary idea because it places the revolution itself in litigation. In effect, if Louis may still be given a trial, he may be absolved, and innocent. What am I to say? He is presumed to be so until he is judged. But if Louis is absolved, if he may be presumed innocent, what becomes of the revolution? If Louis is innocent, all the defenders of liberty become slanderers. Our enemies have been friends of the people and of truth and defenders of innocence oppressed; all the declarations of foreign courts are nothing more than the legitimate claims against an illegal faction. Even the detention that Louis has endured is, then, an unjust vexation; the fédérés, the people of Paris, all the patriots of the French Empire are guilty; and this great trial in the court of nature judging between crime and virtue, liberty and tyranny, is at last decided in favor of crime and tyranny. Citizens, take warning; you are being fooled by false notions; you confuse positive, civil rights with the principles of the rights of mankind; you confuse the relationships of citizens amongst themselves with the connections between nations and an enemy that conspires against it; you confuse the situation of a people in revolution with that of a people whose government is affirmed; you confuse a nation that punishes a public functionary to conserve its form of government, and one that destroys the government itself. We are falling back upon ideas familiar to us, in an extraordinary case that depends upon principles we have never yet applied."

Nevertheless, proponents of holding a trial, if only for show, won out. Louis Capet was brought before the Convention on December 11, and after several days of questioning, he was allowed ten days to prepare his case. In the Tower, the former King prepared for his trial and was given counsel and time to make his preparations, but it was a certainty that the trial would be a sham. On Christmas Day, Louis wrote his will, giving the care of his children to his wife.

The trial began on December 26, 1792, and though Louis' defense was genuine and his counsel quite eloquent, everyone present already knew the outcome. Marat expressed respect for the King's lawyer, but still recognized the necessity of the King's death for the Republic's long-term success. On January 14, the Convention unanimously found the former King guilty. Now it was a matter of how to punish him. Robespierre, who had so stringently opposed the death penalty, now embraced it, and his passionate speeches likely helped to assure the King's death. As

Robespierre himself put it, "It is with regret that I pronounce the fatal truth: Louis must die that the country may live." Of course, the King had to die, not for his crimes, but to preserve the new Republic of France, who feared that a restoration of Louis XVI to the throne was an obvious threat. To critics who pointed out that Robespierre was once such a forceful opponent against the death penalty, he countered,

"As for myself, I abhor the death penalty administered by your laws, and for Louis I have neither love, nor hate; I hate only his crimes. I have demanded the abolition of the death penalty at your Constituent Assembly, and am not to blame if the first principles of reason appeared to you moral and political heresies. But if you will never reclaim these principles in favor of so much evil, the crimes of which belong less to you and more to the government, by what fatal error would you remember yourselves and plead for the greatest of criminals? You ask an exception to the death penalty for him alone who could legitimize it? Yes, the death penalty is in general a crime, unjustifiable by the indestructible principles of nature, except in cases protecting the safety of individuals or the society altogether. Ordinary misdemeanors have never threatened public safety because society may always protect itself by other means, making those culpable powerless to harm it. But for a king dethroned in the bosom of a revolution, which is as yet cemented only by laws; a king whose name attracts the scourge of war upon a troubled nation; neither prison, nor exile can render his existence inconsequential to public happiness; this cruel exception to the ordinary laws avowed by justice can be imputed only to the nature of his crimes. With regret I pronounce this fatal truth: Louis must die so that the nation may live."

When it came to a punishment, the votes varied, but Louis was ultimately sentenced to die by a bare majority (though the exact vote count is unknown). Louis was told of the verdict on the morning of January 17, and on the evening of January 20, he was allowed to meet with Marie Antoinette and his children to say goodbye.

The Execution of Louis XVI

Thus, when Louis Capet, formerly King Louis XVI, once king of the European continent's most powerful nation, climbed the scaffold on January 21, 1793, the guillotine awaited him. As Louis was brought onto the scaffold, he was placed near a pedestal that had previously held a statue of his grandfather, Louis XV. Allowed to speak, Louis told his former subjects, "I die perfectly innocent of the so-called crimes of which I am accused. I pardon those who are the cause of my misfortunes." Though he wished to say more, he was cut off by a drum roll ordered by Antoine-Joseph Santerre, a general in the National Guard. Quickly thereafter, the guillotine was put to use, and some accounts of the execution suggest the guillotine did not successfully behead Louis on the first attempt. Upon his death, as his blood dripped to the ground, people in the crowd rushed forward and dipped handkerchiefs in the former king's blood. For the first and last time in its history, France had executed its king.

After the former King's death, at Danton's insistence, the Convention reestablished the revolutionary tribunal, which consisted of 10 jurors, two substitutes and a public prosecutor and had the ability to sentence people to death. Robespierre, who had accepted the necessity of the death penalty in the King's case, was now willing to apply it to all counter-revolutionaries. As Robespierre would later assert, If the attribute of popular government in peace is virtue, the attribute of popular government in revolution is at one and the same time virtue and terror, virtue without which terror is fatal, terror without which virtue is impotent. The terror is nothing but justice, prompt, severe, inflexible; it is thus an emanation of virtue."

Louis was dead, but the division between the Girondists and Robespierre and his allies only continued to become more pronounced. With that came strife, and when a new wave of insurrection began in Paris, Danton encouraged the formation of the Committee of Public Safety to serve as a temporary government and restore stability. At the same time, the Girondists refused to have anything more to do with Danton, leading to more division.

By April 1793, disputes between the Girondists and Jacobins had reached a new level. The Girondists began to attack not only the Jacobins, but even the Commune. In April and again in May, the Jacobins demanded the expulsion of the Girondons from the Convention. By late May, the people of Paris intervened, and in early June a mob arrived at the Convention to arrest nearly three dozen deputies for counter-revolutionary activities. With that, many of the Girondists fled the city, and those remaining were arrested. The purging of the Girondists was underway.

The Committee of Public Safety was made up of nine deputies, elected each month, and none of those originally chosen for the Committee of Public Safety were Girondists. The Committee for Public Safety not only held significant political power, but, perhaps most importantly, it also controlled the revolutionary tribunal, the primary instrument through which power could be wielded and punishment inflicted.

Meanwhile, work on the constitution continued. Robespierre believed that any constitution must begin with a declaration of rights, not unlike the one in the United States constitution. A new constitutional committee followed the expulsion of the Girondists, and the newly drafted constitution included measures to protect the rights of the poor, create a welfare system and provide state-supported education.

The new constitution was completed, but it was just as quickly suspended because many of France's departments were in open revolt against the republican government. Delegates, including Robespierre's brother Augustin, were sent throughout France to assess the situation.

In early April, Marat was elected President of the Jacobins, a largely symbolic office. Each president served for only ten sessions, but the presidency did signify Marat's importance and status at this time; he had become part of the establishment he had battled so stridently against. Marat would only preside at a single meeting, on April 5, 1793.

As President, Marat signed a declaration, without reading it, that called for the expulsion of the Girondins from the Convention and for patriots from throughout France to enforce the expulsion with force, coming armed to Paris. He was not, in any way, personally involved with the declaration, although he did agree with its content. The paper Marat signed was brought up at the Convention on April 12 and again, an attempt was made to arrest him.

In response to calls for his arrest, Marat suggested that both he and the Girondin leaders be tried by the Tribunal, seemingly illustrating his fundamental belief in the correctness of the

Tribunal. He felt that the Tribunal would see justice done, but the Girondins had planned their attack well. Many members of the Mountain were away on Convention business, and when the motion to try Marat passed, he refused to surrender and escaped.

Marat had significant support in the Jacobins, including Robespierre and even the mayor of Paris offered his support. While Marat avoided Convention sessions, he simply stayed at home with his wife, rather than going into hiding after this call for his arrest, and he agreed to present himself before the Tribunal if he was indicted. The Girondins attempted to indict him the following day and eventually passed an indictment on April 22, while the majority of members of the Mountain were still away from the Convention. Marat presented himself, as he had stated he would, before the tribunal on April 23. He was accompanied by many supporters and allowed to choose his own prison, selecting the Conciergerie.

A remaining part of the Conciergerie

Marat entered the courtroom surrounded by patriotic women throwing flowers. He was introduced as the "people's friend," controlled the trial, and even asked questions from his seat. Marat spoke in his own defense before the Tribunal, maintaining the calm demeanor he consistently showed, and defended himself against each of the charges put forth by the Girondins.

Marat was helped by other factors. For example, there was no prosecuting attorney present, and the charges were quickly conceived and poorly thought out. In one of the charges, Marat was accused of having caused the suicide of a young Englishman, William Johnson, even though Johnson was actually still alive. Famous American pamphlet writer and revolutionary Thomas Paine was also called to speak against Marat, but instead he expressed that his impression of Marat had always been neutral, rather than negative. Marat's trial ended with a long speech condemning the Girondins and accusing them of treason.

He was unanimously acquitted and left the court room carried on the shoulders of his supporters. Paintings and prints showing "The Triumph of Marat" were widely circulated in Paris. While Marat easily avoided the Girondin charges, they had created a dangerous precedent. A member of the Convention could be brought before the Tribunal, and potentially, be condemned to die. Eventually, the Girondins would fall victim to their own precedent.

"Marat's Triumph". A political cartoon depicting Marat carried away by a joyous crowd.

Following Marat's trial, the Girondins established a Commission of Twelve to investigate the Jacobin-dominated Paris Commune. The Girondins may have held power in the Convention, but the Commune was securely in Jacobin hands.

The Commission of Twelve arrested several Parisians, including the Jacques Hebert and the leader of the Enrages, Jean Varlet. The arrests were, according to Marat, intended to provoke violence among the sans-culottes. The Parisian sections called for the Commission to be dismantled, but the Girondin president of the Convention, Maximin Isnard, refused and went so far as to threaten the city of Paris.

On May 26, Marat spoke before the Jacobins, calling for the Jacobins and the Mountain to rise up against the Commission of Twelve. He addressed the Convention the following day and called for insurrection among the sections of Paris on May 30. The tocsin sounded on the morning of May 31, with at least one contemporary account suggesting that Marat, himself, rang the bell.

A delegation from the Paris Commune, supported by Robespierre, demanded the indictment of the Girondins in the Convention on May 31 while a crowd of sans-culottes surrounded the Convention hall. The following day, a prominent Girondin, Jean-Marie Roland, fled Paris, and his wife, prominent in her own right, was arrested. When Marat left the Convention that day, the people shouted to him, "Marat, save us". Marat was called to the Hotel de Ville to help calm the people, but he called for insurrection against the elected officials.

By June 2, a large crowd surrounded the Convention, including both sans-culottes and the National Guard, and the National Guard began to block the exits as many of the delegates attempted to leave. Marat urged them back inside, and Georges Couthon, a member of the Mountain, moved for the arrests of the Girondin leaders. The motion passed, and with that the Jacobins now held full control over the Convention. Those arrested by the Commission of Twelve were freed, but they would later fall during the Reign of Terror.

Marat resigned the day after the insurrection succeeded in indicting the Girondins, so that the Girondins could not use him against the Jacobins to reduce the efficacy of the new government. His resignation was not accepted, but he stopped performing all his duties anyway. Marat's reasons for resigning may have been political, but his health was also failing.

The Assassination of Marat

By June 3, 1793, Marat was quite ill. His skin condition had worsened significantly and he had a respiratory illness as well. Indeed, he rarely left his apartment after giving his resignation to the Convention, spending much of his time in bed or the bath. Though he continued to publish his paper, new articles were rare during this time. The Ami du Peuple now consisted primarily of reprinted articles and letters from readers.

Marat did receive visitors at home and continued to send letters to the Committee for Public Safety and the President of the Convention, acting somewhat like a dignitary. His visitors included deputies from the Jacobins inquiring about his health, but to his surprise, he had lost much of his influence. His former allies now seemingly paid little attention to him, as if he had fully served his function.

Legislative changes in the Convention came by mid-June, including the elimination of all remaining traces of feudalism. The former peasantry now had additional options, as a new working class and part of a capitalist economy. Marat returned to the Convention floor on June 17 and June 18, but he would not leave his home again after that. On July 10, Danton was removed from the Committee for Public Safety. As a moderate, his influence was unwelcome.

On July 4, Marat published an article denouncing the Enrages, calling them false patriots and labeling them a threat to the newly established Jacobin Republic. While he may have personally sympathized with their cause, he believed that their rebellion against the Jacobin Republic could increase support for counterrevolutionaries. He went on to call for the Convention to act to stabilize food prices and control the costs of essential commodities.

A heat wave struck Paris in the second week of July, worsening Marat's skin condition, and his hard work and stress from the prior years likely also increased the inflammation in his skin. As a result, he spent nearly all of his time soaking in a medicated tub, which had a large board and rug over it that provided for his modesty and enabled him to write in the bath. During his final days, Marat regularly greeted visitors from his bath, at least when he was not overly fatigued, and to ensure he had enough rest Simonne limited his visitors.

As it turned out, Simonne was not able to limit the most important visitor of all, who was allowed into Marat's room by Marat himself.

Charlotte Corday

Charlotte Corday was born in 1768 in Normandy to minor nobility, but following the death of her mother and older sister, she was raised in a nearby convent. She was well-read, encountering the works of Voltaire and Rousseau in the convent library. In 1791, she left the convent to live with her cousin, Madame Le Coustellier de Bretteville-Gouville. She was named the sole heir to her cousin's estate in Caen.

While living in Caen, Corday met several of the leaders of the Girondins and began to sympathize with the Girondins. Following their expulsion on June 2, a number of Girondins settled in Caen, and though Corday was sympathetic to the Revolution as a whole, she strongly opposed the Jacobins, who she viewed as radical and violent. Corday did not believe that Louis XVI should have been executed and blamed the Jacobins, particularly Marat, for the September massacres. By the turn of 1793, she feared for a potential civil war.

On July 9, 1793, Corday travelled from Caen to Paris with a mission in mind. She purchased a 6-inch kitchen knife with an ebony handle at a shop in Paris and wrote Addresse aux Français amis des lois et de la paix ("Address to the French people, friends of Law and Peace"), a long explanation for her motives and actions, from her rented room in the city. She went to the Convention, but when she found that Marat no longer attended meetings, she was forced to change her strategy. She may have chosen Marat as a well-known and radical representative of the Jacobins, for his role in the Girondin expulsion, or perhaps because he seemed an easy and accessible target.

When Corday went to Marat's home on July 13, she appeared as a well-dressed young woman with long, chestnut hair. Simonne turned her away. Later in the day, she sent a messenger to Marat claiming to have knowledge of a Girondin conspiracy in Caen. She returned again that evening, with a note requesting an audience the following day tucked into the bosom of her dress, and this time Marat agreed to see her from his bath.

Left alone with Marat, Corday began to provide names of several Girondins supposedly involved in the plot, as Marat dutifully began writing them down. While this was going on, Corday pulled out the knife she had bought and stabbed him right in the heart, piercing his lung, aorta and left ventricle. Marat cried out "Aidez-moi, ma chère amie!" ("Help me, my dear friend!"), but he died almost immediately after the severe stabbing. A surgeon-dentist present nearby bandaged the wound and moved Marat from the bath to his bed, pronouncing him dead at the scene.

Copy of l'Ami du Peuple with Marat's blood on it

Corday was immediately arrested in Marat's home and taken to the nearby Abbaye prison. A crowd gathered around the carriage that took her to prison, jeering and yelling, but Corday remained quite calm through the ride, sitting straight and serene as the National Guard protected her from their potential assaults.

Once she reached the prison, she was isolated, seeing only her jailers, until she was transferred to the Conciergerie before her trial and requested a portrait artist paint her image prior to her execution. The Convention complied, and the portrait was completed after her trial. Corday was reportedly pleased with her likeness. Corday also wrote a letter to her father, saying goodbye.

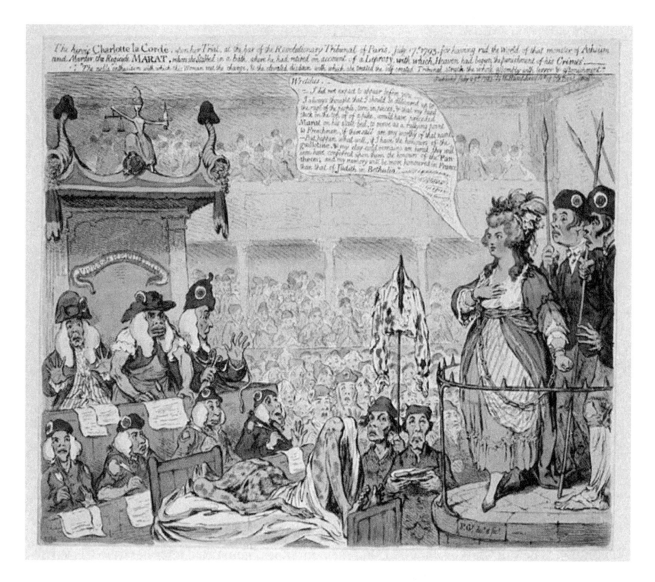

James Gillray's caricature of Corday's trial, 1793

Corday certainly never would've received a fair trial, but one wasn't needed anyway. Corday wholeheartedly confessed that she acted alone at her trial, famously stating, "I killed one man to save a hundred thousand", a clever allusion to a similar remark Robespierre had made in favor of killing Louis XVI.

Only four days later, on the morning of her execution, she was taken to the Salle de la Toilette. Her long hair was cut and she changed into a rough, red shift (symbolizing patricide) before she was taken to the guillotine. It rained on the hour-long journey to the guillotine, but the weather cleared before she reached the guillotine on the cool summer day. Robespierre, Desmoulins and Danton watched the cart pass from a window along the route.

If Corday was nervous or scared that morning, she didn't show it. Corday ran up the stairs before she was led to the guillotine, and when the executioner attempted to block her view of the guillotine, she asked him to step aside because she'd never seen one before. Relatively few women had been guillotined, and there was some concern for feminine sensibilities even at the time of execution, but Corday was calm and seemingly unaffected in the moments leading up to her death.

Moments later, Corday was executed, and following her execution, a hired man who had worked on the guillotine that morning picked up her head and slapped her cheeks. The executioner, Sanson, had attempted to act very respectfully and was horrified, and contemporaries claimed that her face blushed, even after the decapitation.

The Jacobins ordered her body autopsied, likely for the purposes of determining whether she was a virgin (and thus whether she had a male companion and possible accomplice or co-conspirator). However, the autopsy found that Corday was a virgin, indicating that she had likely acted independently. Women had played a small part in the Revolution as a whole to date, but Corday had just made herself one of the most notorious assassins in French history.

While some members of the Convention focused on the trial of Corday and her execution, others immediately began work on Marat's funeral. Given his revolutionary work, and the fact that it had been illicit for much of the early years of the Revolution, it is not a great surprise that Marat died a pauper with only two foreign coins and an assignat worth 25 sous in his possession. Despite his personal finances, his funeral was a grand affair, planned by the painter and revolutionary Jacques-Louis David. The funeral pageant, lit by torches, wound through the streets of Paris for six hours, with cannons firing in the city every five minutes during the six hour procession.

Marat's death mask

While Marat's body was interred, his heart was removed and placed in the Cordeliers' Club, following a second funeral ceremony. His heart was placed into an agate vase, originally the property of the French King. During the funeral orations, he was compared, repeatedly, to Jesus. The urn was suspended from the ceiling of the Cordeliers' Club, and those present swore an oath to avenge Marat.

Fittingly, Marat, who had been all but forgotten around the time of his death, became a saint and martyr in death for the Jacobins. Busts and portraits decorated formal spaces, while many revolutionaries wore medallions bearing his image. Plays, poetry and songs celebrated his life and streets were renamed in honor of him. Montmartre in Paris was now Mont Marat. He was a symbol for the Revolution and the young Jacobin Republic.

Marat, so often called a prophet, had predicted his own assassination in the years prior, and despite his death, the next edition of his journal appeared the following day, dated July 14, 1793. Thus, with impeccable timing, the last issue of the Publiciste de la Republique Francaise was published on the fourth anniversary of the storming of the Bastille. Ironically, this edition featured a harsh criticism of the Committee of Public Safety, and Marat singled out Bertrand Barere in his critique. While Marat had encouraged the formation of the Committee and supported its purpose, he had harbored serious suspicions about some of the members of the Committee. He offered his continued support to Antoine Saint-Just. Robespierre, the man most closely associated with the Committee and the Reign of Terror, was not yet a member.

Saint-Just

Upon Marat's death, radicals in the Convention, Commune and public began vying for Marat's social position and status within revolutionary circles, and several among the Enrages, including Jacques Roux and Leclerc de Lyon, began their own journals. Roux published an edition of the Publiciste de la Republique Francaise and attributed it to Marat's ghost, while Leclerc began a new edition of the Ami du Peuple. Hebert, too, claimed to be Marat's heir, and he was probably a better representative since he was well-regarded by the sans-culottes. The Cordeliers also attempted to publish his work and resurrect his daily political journal, unsuccessfully.

Hebert

While Hebert and others sought Marat's journalistic heritage, his political role was equally desirable.Danton, already excluded from the Committee for Public Safety, claimed that he had long supported Marat, avoiding any mention of his own attempts to maintain a substantial distance between himself and Marat's politics. The leaders of the Mountain, including Robespierre, also staked their rights to Marat's legacy. Robespierre, in particular, took on Marat's role in the Convention.

Before Marat's death, Robespierre had avoided taking a position on the Committee for Public Safety, but he reconsidered and took a seat on the Committee on July 26, 1793. He was, at that time, especially committed to seeing to "food supplies and popular law". The Constitution was finally complete and the Convention could, as had been intended from its beginning, dissolve. On August 11, the Constitution was suspended until such a time as it could be safely implemented. Creating a new constitutional republic during a time of war seemed an unlikely possibility, even to more conservative members of the Convention.

On August 8, at Robespierre's request, the Widow Marat, Simonne Evrard, addressed the Convention. She condemned the Enrages, using Marat's name to further the goals of the Committee of Public Safety. Jacques Roux later committed suicide in prison and Leclerc faded into obscurity. The Jacobins now ruled with absolute power and had no powerful external enemies; only internal conflict within the party remained. While Marat was treated as a martyr, pamphlets and cartoons were also circulating offering a less positive view of the revolutionary. Caricatures and vulgar libels had become common in the city. The Widow Marat spoke against these in front of the Convention. A few weeks later, Marat's sister, Albertine, published a pamphlet denouncing these lies.

The Reign of Terror

After the assassination of Marat, one Girondin leader expressed that Corday had sentenced them to death, but shown them how to die, following her execution. Indeed, the assassination of Marat was all the justification the Jacobins needed for full prosecution of the imprisoned Girondins, and the path was now clear for Robespierre and the Committee of Public Safety to begin its infamous reign of terror. With members of the Jacobins and Cordeliers vowing vengeance for Marat's death, many naturally began to call for the execution of the Girondins, many of whom had already been imprisoned after having been indicted by the Convention. Corday's assassination of Marat made the trial a formality, and the Revolutionary Tribunal sentenced 21 of the Girondins to death, even though all evidence suggested that Corday acted alone without the influence or support of the Girondins in Paris.

While Robespierre took his seat on the Committee in late July, the Terror did not begin until September 5. A popular insurrection on September 4 called for higher wages and more bread, and now faced with pressure from the sans-culottes, the Convention authorized action against hoarders and anyone who was not openly and outwardly patriotic. On September 5, the Convention authorized revolutionary armies, stepped up arms production to arm all of the sans-culottes with muskets. The Revolutionary Tribunal was also divided into several sections, which allowed the Tribunal to hear more cases and allowed for smaller juries to convict the guilty.

Depiction of the Revolutionary Tribunal

That day, in the Convention, Robespierre declared Terror "the order of the day" and defined the Terror as "nothing other than justice; prompt, severe and inflexible". Formerly opposed to the death penalty, Robespierre now believed that harsh action was essential to preserve the Revolution and the young Jacobin Republic. The Terror was embraced by the sans-culottes, whose leader, Pierre Gaspard Chaumette, even called for arming bands of sans-culottes with guillotines on wheels to make the Terror more conveniently portable.

Chaumette

Few were as vocal in their support of Enlightenment ideals as Robespierre, who was heavily versed in Rousseau and Montesquieu, a champion of the bourgeoise, and an advocate of human rights who opposed both slavery and the death penalty. Robespierre was often called the "incorruptible", but in Seeptember 1793, he viewed the world as a clear duality of good and evil. True patriots were good. Anyone who questioned the actions of the Republic was, by definition guilty. The only way to protect and purify the Republic was through the Terror, so the investigative activities of the Committee and judicial activities of the Tribunal increased at once as he gained power.

Robespierre's closest ally on the Committee for Public Safety was Antoine de Saint-Just. The two shared both a passionate belief in the Revolution and significant moral inflexibility. While he was no longer the young man who had opposed the death penalty, he attempted measures to provide help to the poor, mandatory education for boys from five to 12 and for girls from five to 11, and price controls to keep food affordable. The man who organized the Reign of Terror was committed to the good of the people and the Revolution, even if his actions did not effectively promote his goals.

Saint-Just

Legislative changes in the coming days and months increased the range of capital crimes, with the potential for the death penalty. Other legislation simply required proof of patriotism.

Hoarding food was declared a capital crime on July 26. The Law of Suspects was passed on September 17, allowing local committees or neighborhood watches to arrest anyone who showed themselves "by their conduct, their contacts, their words or their writings" to be supporters of tyranny and enemies of the Revolution. Neighbors turned in one another. Crimes as simple as serving sour wine or speaking for a foreign enemy could lead to arrest, conviction and death. Former nobles who were not actively committed to the Revolution could also be arrested. All citizens were required to carry a certificate of civisme, a sort of revolutionary identification card required for a number of legal functions, including acquiring a passport to leave the country. Some people were arrested for the simple crime of using formal rather than informal address and opting for any form of address other than "citizen".

On September 21, women were ordered to wear the tricolor ribbon on their dresses, a measure supported by the Société des Citoyennes Républicaines Révolutionnaires, an organization of revolutionary women. Many women disliked these regulations, particularly as the powerful women's group lost favor in the coming months. Female merchants were particularly offended by these regulations and the actions of the Societe des Citoyennes. While women attempted to organize and play a role in the Revolution, they were not welcomed. Robespierre and others who favored Rousseau firmly believed that women had no public role to play. The Convention banned women's political organizations on October 30, 1793. Chaumette, the leader of the sans-culottes, spoke out in favor of the ban, defining women's role as within the home, not the Revolution.

Additional price controls were introduced to calm the sans-culottes. The General Maximum Law on September 29 allowed any merchant selling goods above the price set by the state to be arrested as well. The Law of 14 Frimaire or the Law of Revolutionary Government passed in December 1793. The Law of 14 Frimaire effectively created a parliamentary dictatorship. Power no longer resided in the Convention, but rather with the Committee for Public Safety. This law reduced any potential for a more moderate perspective.

Cultural policies also accompanied the Terror. The traditional Christian calendar was replaced by a new Republican calendar. In the fall of 1793, the Convention created a committee charged with the development of a new, revolutionary calendar. The calendar consisted of twelve months, renamed after natural events. Each month was divided into three 10-day weeks, called decades. The day was divided into only ten hours, each consisting of one hundred newly defined minutes. The calendar was dated from September 22, 1792 or the creation of the Republic. It was, therefore, already Year II when the calendar was adopted by the revolutionary government. The new calendar eliminated saint's days, religious festivals and the traditional Sunday Sabbath.

One of the first victims of the Reign of Terror was possibly its most famous. Marie Antoinette's "trial" was even more of a sham than her husband's, as the revolutionary government saw the former queen's execution as essential to cement their place and unify the revolutionaries. To that end, the former Queen was accused of a host of trumped up charges, including throwing orgies in Versailles, sending millions of livres to Austria, plotting to assassinate the Duke of Orléans, having her Swiss Guards massacred in 1792, and, worst of all, sexually abusing her son. To that end, her young son was coached by authorities to turn against her and level charges of sexual abuse. While she was allowed legal counsel, she was given less than a day to prepare a defense against charges whose origins came from libelles, the 18th century equivalent of tabloids.

   Antoinette remained composed during the proceedings until pressed about the sexual abuse charge leveled against her. To that point, when asked why she had remained silent regarding that charge, the doting mother countered, "If I have not replied it is because Nature itself refuses to respond to such a charge laid against a mother." After more than 30 hours of trial over two days, Antoinette was convicted and sentenced to death. On October 16, 1793, the former Queen had her hair cut off and was paraded through Paris on an open cart. By now, the former Queen, merely referred to as Widow Capet, was thin, pale, and suffering from serious blood loss as the result of her gynecological difficulties. Nevertheless, she remained quiet and dignified on the cart ride and as she mounted the scaffold, her courage remained intact. Her last words were reputed to have been "Pardon me sir, I meant not to do it", due to the fact she had inadvertently stepped on her executioner's toe while mounting the scaffold. Marie Antoinette was executed shortly after noon, and her remains were dumped in an unmarked grave.

Depiction of Marie Antoinett's Execution

Just days after the execution of the former queen, on October 21, 1793 the Committee ordered that all non-juring priests, those refusing to take an oath to the Revolutionary government, be killed on site. The papacy had disallowed this oath, so to take it was to break with the Church. In the fall of 1793, the Cult of Reason became prominent. Atheists humiliated the clergy and had nuns whipped. Joseph Fouche, a military commander, ordered all Christian ornaments, including crosses and statues, removed from cemeteries. These ornaments were replaced by the words "Death is an eternal sleep". Churches were turned into temples to reason and the journalist Jacques-Rene Hebert and the leader of the sans-culottes Chaumette organized the Fete du Raison in November 1793. The Goddess of Reason was portrayed by a living woman. Accusations of sexual or licentious behavior accompanied these festivals. The Fete du Raison in Paris took place in the Cathedral of Notre Dame.

Altars were dismantled, confessionals melted down for copper for the cannons and the wealth of the Church seized by the state. Many churches became grain or arms storage facilities and a significant number, including Notre Dame de Paris, were damaged or defaced. Protestant churches and Jewish synagogues were also closed in the fall and winter of 1793 as the Cult of Reason grew in prominence in the Convention and Committee. The Archbishop of Paris was forced to wear the red cap associated with the Revolution and many priests were forced to marry. The wealth of the Church provided much of the funds required to maintain the government during the Reign of Terror.

The former Queen's trial and execution occurred only a few weeks into the reign of terror, but Robespierre paid little attention. He was more focused on the trial of the Girondists, which came on October 24, a week after Marie Antoinette's execution. Many of the Girondists had run, hoping to escape the actions of the Committee and tribunal. Brissot was captured and imprisoned. Petion ran, but his body was found, half-eaten by wolves, in a field.

For the Girondists, the necessity of a conviction was immediately apparent to Robespierre. The Jacobins pressed for a trial by conscience. In a trial by conscience, the jury did not have to hear all of the evidence, nor did they have to act based on the evidence. The jury could condemn on the basis of an instinctive response, acting upon their political beliefs. Robespierre supported the very summary nature of such trials, explaining "slowness of judgments is equal to impunity" and "uncertainty of punishment encourages all the guilty". The Girondins, numbering 21 in all, were tried for their crimes against the Convention and executed by guillotine on October 31, 1793. Several of the Girondins had escaped and were hunted down, while those who were not hunted down committed suicide in many cases, including Robespierre's former friend Jean-Marie Roland. In some cases the family and servants of the Girondins were also executed. A number of the Girondins did escape overseas, returning after Robespierre fell and were eventually reinstated as part of the Convention.

Madame Roland

   The city of Lyons, second largest in France and approximately 300 miles east of Paris, was under the control of a Girondin mayor and administration in early 1793. The moderate administration was opposed by the Central Club, which was led by Joseph Chalier, and in February 1793 Chalier called for a Revolutionary Tribunal in the city of Lyons. An insurrection resulted and Chalier and his allies controlled Lyons from March 1793 for a period of 80 days.

Joseph Chalier

ident du Tribunal Révolutionnaire de Lyon

Chalier

The new administration immediately instituted a number of radical revolutionary measures, including a municipal bakery, a forced tax on the wealthy, and a new revolutionary army. While the government's measures attempted to improve conditions for the people, Lyons' finances were in dire straits and bread prices were as much as 30 percent higher than they were in Paris. The municipal government held daily meetings of all civic functionaries, and on May 14, their revolutionary measures were voted down in the daily meeting. Chalier and his allies were arrested by Girondin factions in the city and news of their overthrow reached Paris on June 1. While the Jacobin administration had not provided Chalier with official aid, his actions were in line with the goals of the revolutionary administration.

When news of the arrests of the Girondins in Paris reached Lyons, the Girondist administration that had just reasserted its control in Lyons began to organize a full-blown rebellion. Lyons, along with Marseilles and Bordeaux, called the very authority of the National Convention into question, and additional revolts occurred throughout the south of France. Some of the cities in revolt planned to March on Paris, and in response the National Convention sent troops, the Revolutionary Army of the Alps, to Lyons. The Army of the Alps finished its mission and began to March toward Lyons on August 10, 1793. By September, the Army of the Alps fully encircled the city of Lyons. Food had already been scarce, but now it became nonexistent.

The Convention sent a team to the Lyons hoping for a peaceful solution, including Georges Couthon, a member of the Committee for Public Safety and close political ally of Robespierre's. Couthon negotiated a truce which held from October 3 to October 7. The leaders of the city agreed to negotiate on October 8, the same day that two of the forts guarding the city fell. The city surrendered on October 9. Couthon favored a policy of conciliation, but when it became clear that the city would not be allowed to survive, Couthon requested a transfer. He was replaced by Collot d'Herbois and Joseph Fouche. While the siege itself did not do great physical harm to the city of Lyons, the policy of retribution that followed revealed the official adoption of Terror as a means of government.

Couthon

On October 11, the delegates from the National Convention in Lyon announced that the walls of the city would be destroyed. The following day, an announcement came that much of the city would be destroyed, while industry and the homes of the poor would be preserved. The city was also to be renamed the Ville-Affranchie, and a military commission was created to judge anyone in the military guilty of revolt while a Commission of People's Justice judged all other rebels. By the end of October, 106 military personnel had been executed, along with 79 civilians.

The National Convention appointed a 7-member panel, the Extraordinary Commission, to immediately implement military justice. The Extraordinary Commission took over in late

November. Between the end of November and the middle of December, the Extraordinary Commission put approximately 300 people to death, sometimes even attempting to use large artillery in place of the firing squad or guillotine. By April of 1794, nearly 2,000 citizens of Lyon had been executed, and houses had been burned throughout the city.

Troops went on to besiege Toulon, Bordeaux and Marseillais, but the rebellion in Toulon was effectively brought to an end by a young artillery captain named Napoleon Bonaparte. However, violence and vengeance continued throughout the French countryside, and thousands were killed, including women and children. The population of the entire region of the Vendee was decimated and the death toll may have been as high as 250,000

A young Napoleon Bonaparte

In February of 1794, the conflict between Robespierre and the atheist Hebert came to a head and an end. Hebert, closely allied with the sans-culottes, supported radical revolutionary politics and was believed to be a threat to the Republic. Denounced by Desmoulins, Hebert and his allies were members of a rival political club, the Cordeliers. On March 4, Hebert announced a new insurrection, calling on the sans-culottes to again rise up against the government, but when this attempt at inciting insurrection failed and Hebert and his associates were denounced in the Convention. Hebert had favored something closer to anarchy than a republican government, and now the Hebertistes, including Hebert and Chaumette, were tried before the Convention and executed by guillotine on March 24, 1794.

Robespierre did not only oppose the radical left within the administration, but also those moderates that remained. Danton and a group within the Convention, called the Indulgents, opposed the Terror, encouraging an end to this policy. Danton worked with journalist

Desmoulins in an attempt to achieve these objectives. Accusations of insider trading and financial gain began to circulate; however, many of the accusations against Danton were personal and came directly from Robespierre's own personal notes. Danton was, amongst other things, accused of having told Robespierre that his only knowledge of upright virtue was that which he showed his wife in bed at night. Clearly Danton was not meeting Robespierre's own standards for harsh and unreproachable morality.

Desmoulins, after repeatedly attacking Hebert and the Cordeliers with Robespierre's support, had published an account of Roman history in his newspaper denouncing dictatorship and the Terror. While earlier issues of his paper had been approved by Robespierre, he did not present this edition, with its translation of Tacitus, to Robespierre prior to publication. Desmoulins had provided Robespierre with a link to his younger self, a man who once upon a time might not have approved of the Terror himself, but now Robespierre allowed his former friend to be executed. Robespierre had attended Desmoulin's wedding and was godfather to his son.

Meanwhile, Danton and his allies in the Convention were arrested on March 30, 1794, and the trials took place from early April onward. Danton was a powerful public speaker, and in response to his passionate defense, Antoine de Saint-Just made a motion that the Tribunal could declare a sentence without trial if the defendant failed to show adequate respect for the court and process of justice. Desmoulins was denied the right to call witnesses, including his old school friend Robespierre. Thus, Danton and 14 others, including Desmoulins, were executed in the spring of 1794. Danton's words, on his way to the guillotine, questioned the morality of the policy of Terror and appeared to eternal justice, rather than earthly justice. At their last meeting, Robespierre had asked Danton "Who says anyone innocent has perished?" Robespierre did not attend the execution and shuttered his windows to avoid watching his former friends die.

The death of Danton and his allies gave Robespierre absolute power over the Committee, and thus control over the course of the Revolution and government. The various executive commissions were controlled by his close allies, and he seemed to hold complete power over the Committee for Public Safety. Though some historians have tried to argue that other Committee members exaggerated Robespierre's influence on the Committee to protect their own reputations in subsequent years, most seem to agree that the revolutionary had essentially become a dictator.

Robespierre's paranoia increased in the coming months. On May 22nd, a would-be assassin attempted to kill one of the Committee members, and an attempt on Robespierre's own life followed on May 23 when a young woman by the name of Cécile Renault approached his residence with two small knives. While he had feared for his life in the past, now the threat was concrete, and yet Robespierre seemed pleased to have been judged threat enough to merit assassination. There were even suspicions that he arranged the attacks.

That said, Robespierre's obsession with conspiracies and counterrevolutionaries had increased substantially even before the assassination attempts. Within hours of Danton and Demoulins' execution, he returned to the Jacobins and promoted Martial Hermann to the Commission for Civil Administration and Police. Hermann was, like Robespierre and Saint-Just, a strict moralist. While the Commission for Civil Administration and Police had broad powers, it also oversaw the day to day management of the Revolutionary Tribunal.

Other political appointments followed as Robespierre created an administration he believed he could trust. Within the next decadi (week) by the new calendar, foreigners and former nobles were expelled from Paris and the surrounding area, as news of rebellion and atrocities from the Vendee, including mass executions, continued to trouble the Convention and Robespierre. Robespierre was absent from both the Jacobins and the Convention for three weeks in the late spring. He may have travelled during this time, possibly to visit one of Rousseau's retreats, or he may have been ill from stress and strain. Contemporaries in the Convention remarked that he was unusually calm upon his return, displaying fewer nervous tics. In late April, Saint-Just set up the Police Bureau, an entity, like the Committee for Public Safety, with the right to issue arrest warrants. Robespierre took control of the Police Bureau in early May and progressively devoted more of his attention to his duties there.

As Robespierre continued his reign of terror, he also began to set forth new doctrines for the French Republic. Robespierre had recognized the importance of religion, both in his personal life and for the state, for some time, and he had clearly harbored no love for Hebert's positions. Now, he began to set forth the doctrine of the Supreme Being. For Robespierre, there was no conflict between his belief in a religion of his own creation and the morality of terror. During one of his last conversations with Danton, he asked, "And who says anyone innocent has perished?" On April 7, the Convention approved a decree establishing the worship of the Supreme Being, including Sabbaths every 10 days, according to the new revolutionary calendar. The first public festival was scheduled for the 8th of June. Throughout Paris, churches were adorned with announcements and doctrines of the new state religion.

Robespierre himself introduced a new religion to the French Republic, speaking before the Convention in May 1794. While he had always retained faith, personally, what he now proposed went far beyond personal faith. Robespierre strongly believed in the essential importance of faith for the people, opposing atheists in the Revolution. He also opposed the control the Church had held over the French government, as well as the policies of the Church. While atheists remained in the Convention, the execution of Hebert and his allies had paved the way for Robespierre's introduction of a state religion. His solution was to create a new state religion.

Robespierre envisioned a deist state religion, called the cult of the Supreme Being. The cult of the Supreme Being recognized the existence of deity and the immortality of the soul. From the first speech at the Convention, it was clear that in Robespierre's mind the worship of the Supreme Being and policy of Terror were completely compatible. During his speech, Robespierre veered from the subject of the Supreme Being to again attack the recently guillotined Danton.

The worship of the Supreme Being was both political and moral. Duty was stressed, as well as patriotism. While the cult included the expectation that one would do good works and defend the oppressed, it also made punishing tyrants and traitors a religious act. New policies and festivals promoted the cult of the Supreme Being, including Sabbath-like celebrations on the decadis or the tenth day of each 10-day week. These festivals celebrated moral virtues and praiseworthy individuals, ranging from friendship, temperance and modesty to the martyrs of freedom, our ancestors and the benefactors of mankind. Family life mattered and was reflected in decadis devoted to mother love, youth, conjugal fidelity and filial piety.

On June 4, 1794, Robespierre was elected president of the Convention. This enabled him to lead the rites and rituals of the new Cult of the Supreme Being at the first Festival of the Supreme Being. Robespierre ran and celebrated the first festival of the Supreme Being on June 8, 1794 or 20 Prairial in the new Revolutionary Calendar. Stage sets were designed by Convention member and artist Jacques-Louis David, who had designed Marat's funeral and painted the best-known image of his death. Homes throughout Paris were decorated with flowers, wreaths and tricolor ribbons and flags. The guillotine had been moved out of the center of the city for the festival.

Robespierre wore a fine, light blue coat and an oversize tricolor sash. Like the other deputies to the convention, he carried a large posy made of flowers and corn. Nearly half a million Parisians, almost the entire population of the city, came to the Festival of the Supreme Being. Robespierre organized a ritual, complete with a symbolic burning of atheism, and he gave a speech that supported many deistic ideals. The deputies of the Convention, seated behind him, were more amused than respectful, and colleague Jacques-Alexis Thuriot was heard saying, "Look at the bugger; it's not enough for him to be master, he has to be God."

While this day seemed optimistic, deputies behind Robespierre snickered at the rituals and the worst of the Terror was still to come.

As Robespierre prepared for the festival, there were two attempts made on his life. While he had long feared assassination, particularly after the death of Marat the previous year, these attempts increased his fear and paranoia. More and more, Robespierre appointed only those he felt her could personally trust to positions of power. From May onward, he spent much of his time at the Police Bureau, reviewing reports of illegal and counterrevolutionary activity. Each case was summarized by his staff and personally decided by him. In some cases, he ordered an arrest warrant. In others, he requested additional information.

Robespierre may have seemingly ignored the behavior of those who mocked him at the festival on June 8, but he soonafter acted in the Convention. June 10, 1794 brought significant legal changes, enabling Robespierre to condemn many more to death. Trials were reduced to mere condemnations and counsel was denied the accused. He created a new category of criminal, simply called "enemies of the people".

These laws were passed without discussion or debate. "Enemies of the People" was a broad category, encompassing nearly anyone and everyone. Crimes could range from serving sour wine to attempting to send letters to England. Only a single punishment was dictated, regardless of the specifics: death. Moreover, proof was not required to sentence someone to death. While the Committee of Public Safety and Committee of General Security had, previously, been the only bodies able to indict, now the Convention, the prosecutor, and provincial representatives could accuse and indict anyone. The Law of 22 Prairial, as it was called, would serve to eliminate any antipatriotic sentiment. It could also be applied to stamp out depravity, forcing Paris to live according to Robespierre's own strict moral code.

While the Reign of Terror had maintained at least a facade of justice before June 10, 1794, the Law of 22 Prairial changed that. There was no longer any requirement of evidence to convict. Simply thinking something against the Revolution could merit the death penalty. A facial expression or lack of action could lead to the guillotine. Juries no longer had to look at evidence, but could simply make a judgment based on perception and morality. Trials were dramatically shorter. A single punishment now sufficed for nearly every crime, ranging from spreading false news to insulting morality. Citizens not only had the right to denounce anyone guilty of any sort of crime against the Republic, but were obligated to do so. A failure to report on a neighbor or acquaintance was guilt by association. All depravity, lack of patriotism and even apathy had to be forcibly removed from the Republic under Robespierre. These new regulations would lead to the death of 1376 individuals in Paris in a period of just 47 days. More of those executed during this phase of the terror were wealthy bourgeoisie, former nobles or clergy than during past months; however, the majority continued to be ordinary French citizens.

While there are no records of the Committee of Public Safety meetings during this time, they were so argumentative that they had to close the windows to avoid being heard. Eventually, the meeting was moved to rooms on an upper floor of the Tuileries for additional privacy. Robespierre and Saint-Just clashed particularly with Lazare Carnot, a military officer. While Carnot was achieving success on the battlefield, Robespierre was suspicious of him. And though Robespierre's actions were extreme, the Terror was in line with the official goals and policies of both the Committee for Public Safety and the Convention. In fact, the Committee of General Security, another body of the Convention, was quite angered at not being involved in the Law of 22 Prairial. Nevertheless, the French began to question the wisdom and justness of these decrees. Robespierre was finally starting to overstep his bounds.

Altogether, 1285 people would die by the guillotine between the 10th of June and 28th of July. In comparison, 269 people were executed between September 1793 and February 1794. While many were executed, 190 were also acquitted during this five-month period. A policy of terror may have existed, but it required Robespierre's influence to reach extremes, sending more people before the Tribunal than ever before. The law now supported the guillotine for even the merest potential of counter-revolutionary thought.

The End of the Terror

Following the introduction of the Cult of the Supreme Being, some members of the Convention began working against Robespierre. He had a number of enemies, including many of the remaining atheists in the Convention, Jean-Lambert Tallien and Joseph Fouche. Tallien and Fouche, both atheists, had been involved in suppressing the rebellion in the Vendee and Lyon and were implicated in the atrocities in those areas. Robespierre had implied, in a speech to the Jacobins on June 11, that they were among the next he planned to arrest and guillotine. Thus, Robespierre's enemies, particularly in the atheist faction in the Convention, planned to take advantage of his support of the Cult of the Supreme Being.

Tallien

Fouche

However, Robespierre was not called the incorruptible for no reason. History may find plenty of fault with Robespierre's methods and extremist ideology, but he had truly earned his nickname, the "Incorruptible"; there was no potential for an actual scandal, so one was concocted in an attempt to remove the dictatorial Robespierre from power. Opponents attempted to link Robespierre to a messianic cult led by Catherine Theot. A letter was created, supposedly dictated by the illiterate old mystic, congratulating Robespierre.

The night before the conspirators intended to reveal the letter to the Committee of General Security, Robespierre was told of it in the Committee for Public Safety. Just a few days later, the falsified letter from Theot to Robespierre appeared and was presented before the Committee of Public Safety. Robespierre argued with another member of the Committee and was called a tyrant. In offense, Robespierre declared that he would not return to the Committee, but in fact he continued to serve as the president of the Convention and signed many documents for the Committee of Public Safety until June 19.

When Robespierre formally resigned on the 19th of June, he still retained significant power in the government and over the guillotine.

Following his resignation as president of the Convention and his departure from the Committee of Public Safety, Robespierre focused all of his attention on the Police Bureau. His staff was increased and work hours lengthened. As head of the Police Bureau, Robespierre personally read through reports and made recommendations. In some cases, he asked for additional information, but more often, he simply rubberstamped the arrest. The Revolutionary Tribunal continued to hold judicial power and was responsible for sentencing the accused to death, and Robespierre appointed his own landlord, Maurice Duplay, to the Revolutionary Tribunal. Other committees were also filled with trusted friends and acquaintances, even after he stepped down as President of the Committee for Public Safety and the Convention.

On June 17, 1794, a group of 61 individuals was executed, making this the largest mass execution in Paris to this date. This group included Robespierre's attempted assassin and several members of her family, the Sainte-Amaranthe family, a young servant girl and a number of others. No one knew what crime the Sainte-Amaranthe family had committed and the crowd railed against the execution of the young girl. Contemporary accounts both blamed Robespierre for these executions and stated that he had fought against them. There were only four days in the month that followed with fewer than 28 executions and one day, July 7, when the total reached 67. The public prosecutor was often awakened during the night with news of additional planned executions the following day.

Around the end of June, Saint-Just returned from the battlefield on the borders of France to assist Robespierre. He brought good news from the battlefield: French troops had won a decisive victory against the Austrians. Some began to call for the institution of the constitution and an end to the war government, but Robespierre, regardless of his now-reduced role in government, believed that the war government needed to remain in power and eliminate internal enemies. From the end of June onward, Robespierre spent much of his time in his rooms, with Saint-Just running back and forth to get his input on Police Bureau cases. This would be the last month of the Terror and the bloodiest.

Robespierre continued his work with the Police Bureau and attended meetings of the Jacobins. He continued to encourage paranoia among the Jacobins; however, his speeches became progressively less effective and less rational. When the anniversary of the storming of the Bastille arrived on July 14, a number of city sections and committees organized simple, fraternal banquets, and some of Robespierre's own allies participated in these banquets. They were, even to the most radical, generally considered acceptable and respectful, but Robespierre disagreed, instead attending the Jacobins and denouncing Fouche again. The Jacobins accommodated Robespierre and expelled Fouche from the meeting and the club. On July 16, Robespierre criticized the banquets held in commemoration of Bastille Day, calling even these simple celebrations unacceptable in the face of current challenges. He went on to accuse those who had participated in supporting counterrevolutionary thoughts. Many of those who attended sent Robespierre apologetic letters, hoping to avoid any possible punishment.

By late July, Robespierre only left his rooms to attend the Jacobins, but he made an exception on July 23 by attending the meeting of the Committee of General Security. He appeared willing to consider compromise at this meeting; however, appearances were deceiving. Robespierre again secluded himself for several days following the meeting and consulted no one.

On July 26, Robespierre attended the daily meeting of the Convention for the first time in weeks. During his three days at home, Robespierre had prepared a very long speech. He presented his speech before the Convention, spending two hours at the podium. Robespierre defended all of his actions, defining himself as one who had been unfairly blamed and persecuted. He spoke against "tyrants, men of blood and oppressors of patriotism". In his speech, he defended the Committee of Public Safety and Committee of General Security, insisting that neither Committee had condemned anyone to die, nor had he, himself. The Committees were simply responsible for charging people, and the responsibility for their deaths was placed solidly with the Revolutionary Tribunal, an argument that convinced nobody.

Like many of Robespierre's speeches, this one had a distinctly personal tone. He seemed offended by accusations of tyranny, identified himself and his personal virtue with the Revolution, and, in this speech, connected personal threats to him, including Jean-Lambert Tallien and Joseph Fouche, with threats to the Revolution. He criticized the plot involving Catherine Theot and its supporters. His speech turned from critical to joyful in reference to the cult of the Supreme Being and the festival of June 8.

Robespierre went on to justify the continuation of the Terror, and though the speech was intended to exonerate him personally, he continued his condemnation of potential spies and counterrevolutionaries in it. While he did not name names in his speech, he insinuated the guilt of a number of members of the Convention, including Fouche and Tallien. Robespierre broadly criticized the Convention for barring the adoption of the Cult of the Supreme Being and directly condemned the atheists in the Convention.

Robespierre was stunned when the Convention reacted with anger and suspicion to his speech. The master rhetorician had spellbound audiences for several years, and he had expected a warm welcome and immediate publication of his speech throughout Paris. Copies of the speech were provided to both Committees by the Convention at once. Then, the unshakeable and incorruptible said the words he had left unspoken, "My speech is to be sent to be examined by the very deputies I accuse!" In his speech, Robespierre had left most of his accusations clouded in vague terms, rather than making clear accusations, but this statement proved that he did, in fact, accuse many on the committee of crimes against the Revolution. Members of the Convention as a whole and the two committees began to denounce Robespierre for his words and actions. Bertrand Barere made an optimistic speech, distracting the Convention from Robespierre and perhaps, preventing his arrest.

Robespierre went to the Jacobins that night and as he expected, found support. His supporters forced two of his opponents out of the club that night. One of Robespierre's closest allies, Saint-Just, had not gone to the Jacobins that night. Saint-Just had gone to the Tuileries and sat in the Committee of Public Safety meeting room. Others, including Collot d'Herbois, one of those driven from the Jacobins, had also come to the Tuileries. Saint-Just agreed to allow the committee to read his speech before giving it before the Convention but had changed his mind before dawn, perhaps after consulting with Robespierre.

On July 27, 1794, Robespierre and Saint-Just entered the Convention together. They had only a few committed allies remaining in the Convention, including Robespierre's brother Augustin and Couthon. As Saint-Just began to give his speech in support of Robespierre, Jean-Lambert Tallien interrupted him, and as members began to hurl accusations at Robespierre and Saint-Just, Saint-Just became silent. Robespierre attempted to speak but was also drowned out, and one deputy, Marc-Guillaume Alexis Vadier, openly mocked him. When Robespierre didn't respond, another deputy shouted, "The blood of Danton chokes him!"

The current president of the Convention, Collot d'Herbois, now refused to allow either Robespierre or Saint-Just speak, and Tallien and Fouche retained control of the floor. Cries of "Down with the tyrant!" echoed in the chamber, and the Convention voted to arrest Robespierre. Augustin volunteered to be arrested alongside Robespierre, and Couthon, Saint-Just, Frances Hanriot and Philippe-Francois-Joseph Le Bas were also arrested.

The five men were allowed to choose their prisons, as a gesture of respect. Le Bas was even allowed time to return home and say goodbye to his wife and collect his things. But Robespierre still had supporters, and they were not about to allow the arrested men to go to the guillotine without a fight. Soldiers from the Commune under General Coffinhal were rounded up to free the prisoners and march against the Convention itself, and in response the Convention ordered its own troops to be called out for a potential confrontation. It was at this point that the Commune's soldiers were withdrawn to the Hôtel de Ville, Paris' City Hall, where Robespierre and his supporters had also gathered and locked themselves into a room. They remained there throughout the night, sending messages out through loyal couriers. 13 sections of Paris sent armed men to protect them, but the remainder did not. Meanwhile, the Convention imposed a sentence of death without trial on Robespierre, Augustin, Saint-Just, Couthon and Le Bas.

Sometime after midnight on July 28, likely around 2:00 a.m., on the orders of the Convention to take the arrested men dead or alive, members of the National Guard forcibly entered the room. During the chaos that followed, Robespierre was shot in the lower jaw, a wound that was likely self-inflicted by a pistol Le Bas had given to him after bringing back a pair of pistols from his home. Le Bas had shot himself with one as the Convention's men entered the room, successfully committing suicide, and it is likely that he gave Robespierre the second. Though it's widely believed Robespierre had unsuccessfully attempted suicide, some eyewitnesses claim he was shot by Charles-André Merda, one of the gendarmes who entered the Hotel de Ville. Augustin attempted to escape through the window but fell to the ground below, breaking his legs and making it easy for him to be taken back into custody. Hanriot jumped out a window, badly injuring himself as well, and it was said he was found unconscious the next day. Couthon pulled himself from his wheelchair and fell down the stairs, suffering a blow to the head but not killing himself. Saint-Just was the only one who did not attempt escape or suicide.

Depiction of Gendarme Merda shooting at Robespierre

After their capture, Saint-Just, Couthon and Robespierre were taken to the meeting room of the Committee of Public Safety. In the early morning hours a surgeon was called to bandage Robespierre's wound and remove several teeth. Adding insult to injury, by late morning the five were called before the Revolutionary Tribunal and sentenced to death. The men who had been arrested again, the corpses of those who had killed themselves, and 17 of those loyal to Robespierre were loaded onto carts and taken to the guillotine. The guillotine, formerly outside the city center, had been returned to the center of the city for the public spectacle.

An enormous crowd gathered to witness the executions. Three carts in total held 22 men that day, including Robespierre, Augustin, and Saint-Just. The cart stopped outside the Duplay home, where Robespierre had taken up residence years earlier, and someone threw a bucket of animal blood on the door. People along the route to the guillotine cursed Robespierre.

All of those involved were guillotined, including the bodies of the dead. Robespierre was the second to last executed. He walked, weakly, up the stairs to the guillotine on his own power rather than being carried. He wore the fine sky blue coat and tricolor sash he had worn on the 8th of June, his happiest day. Robespierre removed his coat and his hands were bound. He remained silent until the executioner ripped the bandage from his shattered face. There is no way to know whether the executioner acted out of simple practicality or cruelty; however, the reports of that day state that Robepierre let out a horrible scream, not unlike a wounded animal. The anguish was only silenced once the blade fell, ending Robespierre's life and making him one of the

Terror's victims. It was July 28, 1794, the last day of the Reign of Terror.

The execution of Robespierre. The beheaded man is not Robespierre, but Couthon; Robespierre is shown sitting on the cart closest to the scaffold, holding a handkerchief to his mouth.

The remaining days of the French Revolution are referred to as the Thermidorian Reaction, after 9 Thermidor or July 27. Prominent figures in the Convention included Tallien, Fouche and Paul Barras. A number of new policies were put into place immediately after the execution of Robespierre and his allies. The Convention's committees continued to exist, but a new rule required that one-quarter of the members resign each month. They were not eligible for immediate reaction.

On August 1, the Committees revoked the Law of 22 Prairial. The Revolutionary Tribunal was purged and the prosecutor, Fouquier-Tinville, arrested on August 10. Counterrevolutionary actions now had to be proven with evidence before the Tribunal. The Watch Committees throughout Paris were gradually eliminated.

Of course, the responsibilities and powers of the Committee of Public Safety were dramatically reduced. It lost all executive powers, retaining only control over war and foreign relations. Only six people were guillotined in August and only 40 total for the rest of the year. Prisoners were released from jail, numbering 3,500 from Paris alone. The Terror had ended.

Both the extreme left and right wing had opposed Robespierre and supported his execution, and the Thermidorians continued to work against the Jacobins. Gangs of "gilded youth," well-dressed young men, harassed Jacobins and other associated with Robespierre, while some released prisoners engaged in anti-Jacobin violence. On October 16, the Convention ordered the release of lists of members of political clubs and forbade correspondence between clubs, a measure intended to reduce the strength of the network of Jacobin clubs. When an attack on a Jacobin club resulted in multiple injuries, the club itself was closed as an incitement to violence. In December 1794, a group of 71 Girondins regained their positions in the Convention. These survivors of the Girondin executions had escaped punishment in 1793.

On November 23, Jean-Baptiste Carrier was brought before the Revolutionary Tribunal. Carrier had been responsible for substantial atrocities while attempting to put down rebellion in Nantes. While in Nantes, Carrier, a Jacobin, ordered the drowning of as many as 4,000 people, including women and children. Carrier claimed he had only been following the orders of the Committee of Public Safety and the Convention as a whole, but he was sentenced to die by the guillotine on December 16, 1794.

Depictions of the drownings at Nantes

While the Terror came to an end with Robespierre's death in July 1794, the end result was not exactly peace. Economic conditions continued to worsen throughout the end of 1794. Food was not only expensive, but extremely scarce in some areas. On December 24, price controls were eliminated, recreating the free market. The winter of 1794 to 1795 was especially bad. While wheat and rice were purchased and subsidized to prevent starvation, fuel shortages worsened the situation. The government went into debt to provide bread rations, but those were becoming less accessible by the spring of 1795. By May of 1795, driven by hunger, the sans-culottes began to organize once again. Bread rations had been cut to as little as one-quarter pound each day. A brief and unsuccessful attempt to call for an insurrection to put the constitution of 1793 and additional bread rations into place followed.

Anti-Jacobin campaigns continued throughout 1795. Marat, who had been treated as a martyr for the cause after his assassination, was now disgraced, and his remains were removed from the Pantheon. Though the sans-culottes protested, Marat's remains have never been found. Remaining Jacobins in the Convention were arrested following the insurrection in May. Several were executed and a number of others committed suicide. While the sans-culottes had demanded a constitution, the new government saw no possibility for the introduction of the 1793 constitution. Royalist factions continued to hope for the return of a constitutional monarchy; however, Louis Charles died in June of the 1795. The former King's brother declared himself to be Louis XVIII; however, he immediately announced the return of traditional royalist policies, including the three Estates and the return of the Church. Even staunch royalists would not support him.

There were substantial legislative and judicial changes throughout 1795. Those who had left the country, including sailors and federalists, were allowed to return to France. A policy of religious freedom was instituted in the spring of 1795; however, religion was to remain entirely private and be kept well out of sight. Several members of the old administration were tried and convicted, but exiled rather than executed.

A number of lynch mobs and murder gangs formed throughout the country. These groups sought vengeance for the crimes associated with the Terror, ranging from official ones, including executions by guillotine, to the deaths caused in Lyons and elsewhere. Called the "White Terror," these gangs sought vengeance, but were minimally organized and did not have political power. Many of these gangs were made up of well-dressed youth, like the gilded youth of Paris. On April 10, legal officials ordered the arrest of a number of suspects associated with the Reign of Terror, possibly as many as 80,000 to 90,000 people. Lynch mobs attacked a number of prisons, killing the prisoners.

Once it was clear that the constitution of 1793 was unacceptable, work began on a new constitution. The constitution of 1795 established a representative democracy with a bicameral legislature and created a Directory to hold executive powers. The executive branch could eliminate freedom of the press and held a number of other powers. Broad taxation supported the government.

The new constitution was a much less egalitarian one than Robespierre would have envisioned or supported. While wealth was not returned to the Church, the distinction between social classes, particularly between property owners and non-land owners, was clear in the new constitution. During the weeks following the completion of the constitution but before it went into effect, the Convention passed a rule stating that two-thirds of the members of the new Assembly had to have served in the Convention. The rule was intended to maintain stability and preserve the Republic, but conservatives rebelled. A young general, Napoleon Bonaparte was assigned to suppress the conservative rebellion and maintain the power of the Convention. Hundreds were killed.

The new constitution for the French Republic took effect on October 26, 1795. The National Guard, loyal to the people, was replaced by an armed force loyal to the government. The Place de la Revolution, where Louis XVI and Marie Antoinette (and nearly 2800 others) were executed, was renamed the Place de la Concorde. The young general who had dealt with the conservative rebels now was made commander-in-chief of the armed forces. Napoleon Bonaparte would, in just a few short years, become first consul-in-chief and later Emperor, bringing an end to the short-lived Republic. Moreover, Robespierre's excesses drew sympathy toward his opponents, and some historians have asserted that the Restoration that followed Napoleon's downfall was made possible in part by the Reign of Terror.

Without question, Robespierre would have been horrified at the results. Personally, he remains one of the most enigmatic and contradictory figures of the French Revolution and French history in general. It is understandably difficult to reconcile the fact that Robespierre lived such a conservatively moral lifestyle, heartily advocated the most democratic notions of natural rights and representative government, and yet engaged in one of Europe's most tyrannical periods in history. Perhaps it is best to summarize Robespierre's life and actions as taking an "ends justify the means" philosophy to an extreme. In that, Robespierre is hardly alone, and even one of America's most revered Founding Fathers and political theorists, Thomas Jefferson, seemed to agree with such a sentiment. An avid supporter of the French Revolution, even during the greatest extremes of the Reign of Terror, Jefferson remarked, "The tree of liberty must be refreshed from time to time with the blood of patriots and tyrants. It is its natural manure."

Over two centuries removed from the Reign of Terror, Robespierre is mostly cast as a villain and an example of a revolutionary who, once he comes to power, becomes more dictatorial than the ruler he rebelled against. With that said, though Robespierre continues to have plenty of detractors, he also continues to elicit some sympathy from certain historians. As Marxist historian Albert Soboul wrote, "Robespierre's main ideal was to ensure the virtue and sovereignty of the people. He disapproved of any acts which could be seen as exposing the nation to counter-revolutionaries and traitors, and became increasingly fearful of the defeat of the Revolution. He instigated the Terror and the deaths of his peers as a measure of ensuring a Republic of Virtue; but his ideals went beyond the needs and wants of the people of France. He became a threat to what he had wanted to ensure and the result was his downfall."

Online Resources

Other books about French history by Charles River Editors

Other books about the French Revolution on Amazon

Further Reading

Abray, Jane (1975). "Feminism in the French Revolution". The American Historical Review. 80 (1): 43–62. doi:10.2307/1859051. JSTOR 1859051.

Andress, David (2006). The Terror: The Merciless War for Freedom in Revolutionary France. Farrar Straus Giroux. ISBN 978-0-374-27341-5.

Baker, Michael (1978). "French political thought at the accession of Louis XVI". Journal of Modern History. 50 (2): 279–303. doi:10.1086/241697. JSTOR 1877422. S2CID 222427515.

Baker, Keith (1995). Van Kley, Dale (ed.). The Idea of a Declaration of Rights in The French Idea of Freedom: The Old Regime and the Declaration of Rights of 1789. Stanford University Press. ISBN 978-0-8047-2355-8.

Barton, HA (1967). "The Origins of the Brunswick Manifesto". French Historical Studies. 5 (2): 146–169. doi:10.2307/286173. JSTOR 286173.

Davidson, Ian (2016). The French Revolution: From Enlightenment to Tyranny. Profile Books. ISBN 978-1846685415.

Beckstrand, Lisa (2009). Deviant women of the French Revolution and the rise of feminism. Fairleigh Dickinson University Press. ISBN 978-1611474008.

Bell, David Avrom (2007). The First Total War: Napoleon's Europe and the Birth of Warfare as We Know It. Mariner Books. ISBN 978-0-618-91981-9.

Bell, David A. (2004). "Class, consciousness, and the fall of the bourgeois revolution". Critical Review. 16 (2–3): 323–351. doi:10.1080/08913810408443613. S2CID 144241323.

Betros, Gemma (2010). "The French Revolution and the Catholic Church". History Today (68).

Blanning, Timothy C. W (1997). The French Revolution: Class War or Culture Clash?. Palgrave Macmillan. ISBN 978-0-333-67064-4.

Blanning, Timothy C. W. (1996). The French Revolutionary Wars: 1787–1802. Hodder Arnold. ISBN 978-0-340-64533-8.

Bredin, Jean-Denis (1988). Sieyes; la clé de la Révolution française (in French). Fallois.

Brezis, Elise S; Crouzet, François (1995). "The role of assignats during the French Revolution: An evil or a rescuer?". Journal of European Economic History. 24 (1).

Brown, Howard G (2006). Ending the French Revolution: Violence, Justice, and Repression from the Terror to Napoleon. University of Virginia Press. ISBN 978-0-8139-2546-2.

Brown, Howard G. (1995). War, Revolution, and the Bureaucratic State Politics and Army Administration in France, 1791-1799. OUP. ISBN 978-0-19-820542-5.

Cerulo, Karen A. (1993). "Symbols and the world system: national anthems and flags". Sociological Forum. 8 (2): 243–271. doi:10.1007/BF01115492. S2CID 144023960.

Censer, Jack; Hunt, Lynn (2001). Liberty, Equality, Fraternity: Exploring the French Revolution. Pennsylvania State University Press. ISBN 978-0-271-02088-4.

Censer, Jack (2002). Klaits, Joseph; Haltzel, Michael (eds.). The French Revolution after 200 Years in Global Ramifications of the French Revolution. Cambridge UP. ISBN 978-0-521-52447-6.

Chanel, Gerri (2015). "Taxation as a Cause of the French Revolution: Setting the Record Straight". Studia Historica Gedansia. 3.

Chapman, Jane (2005). "Republican citizenship, ethics and the French revolutionary press". Ethical Space: The International Journal of Communication Ethics. 2 (1).

Chisick, Harvey (1993). "The pamphlet literature of the French revolution: An overview". History of European Ideas. 17 (2): 149–166. doi:10.1016/0191-6599(93)90289-3.

Chisick, Harvey (1988). "Pamphlets and Journalism in the Early French Revolution: The Offices of the Ami du Roi of the Abbé Royou as a Center of Royalist Propaganda". French Historical Studies. 15 (4): 623–645. doi:10.2307/286549. JSTOR 286549.

Clark, J.C.D. (2000). English Society: 1660–1832; Religion, Ideology and Politics During the Ancient Regime. Cambridge University Press. ISBN 978-0-521-66627-5.

Clark, Samuel (1984). "Nobility, Bourgeoisie and the Industrial Revolution in Belgium". Past & Present. 105 (105): 140–175. doi:10.1093/past/105.1.140. JSTOR 650548.

Cobban, Alan (1964). The Social Interpretation of the French Revolution (1999 ed.). Cambridge University Press. ISBN 978-0521661515.

Cole, Alistair; Campbell, Peter (1989). French electoral systems and elections since 1789.

ISBN 978-0-566-05696-3.

Comninel, George C (1987). Rethinking the French Revolution: Marxism and the Revisionist Challenge. Verso. ISBN 978-0-86091-890-5.

Cook, Bernard A (2004). Belgium (Studies in Modern European History, V. 50). Peter Lang Publishing Inc. ISBN 978-0820458243.

Conner, Clifford (2012). Jean-Paul Marat: Tribune of the French Revolution. Pluto Press. ISBN 978-0-7453-3193-5.

Cough, Hugh (1987). "Genocide and the Bicentenary: the French Revolution and the Revenge of the Vendee". Historical Journal. 30 (4): 977–988. doi:10.1017/S0018246X00022433. S2CID 159724928.

Crook, Malcolm (1996). Elections in the French Revolution: An Apprenticeship in Democracy, 1789-1799. Cambridge University Press. ISBN 978-0-521-45191-8.

Crowdy, Terry (2004). French Revolutionary Infantry 1789–1802. Osprey. ISBN 978-1-84176-660-7.

Crowe, Ian (2005). An Imaginative Whig: Reassessing the Life and Thought of Edmund Burke. University of Missouri Press. ISBN 978-0-8262-6419-0.

Dalton, Susan (2001). "Gender and the Shifting Ground of Revolutionary Politics: The Case of Madame Roland". Canadian Journal of History. 36 (2): 259–282. doi:10.3138/cjh.36.2.259. PMID 18711850.

Dann, Otto; Dinwiddy, John (1988). Nationalism in the Age of the French Revolution. Continuum. ISBN 978-0-907628-97-2.

Delon, Michel; Levayer, Paul-Édouard (1989). Chansonnier révolutionnaire (in French). Éditions Gallimard. ISBN 2-07-032530-X.

Desan, Suzanne; Hunt, Lynn; Nelson, William (2013). The French Revolution in Global Perspective. Cornell University Press. ISBN 978-0801450969.

Devance, Louis (1977). "Le Féminisme pendant la Révolution Française". Annales Historiques de la Révolution Française (in French). 49 (3).

Dorginy, Marcel (2003). The Abolitions of Slavery: From L.F. Sonthonax to Victor Schoelcher, 1793, 1794, 1848. Berghahn Books. ISBN 978-1571814326.

Doyle, William (1990). The Oxford History of the French Revolution (2002 ed.). Oxford

University Press. ISBN 978-0-19-160829-2.

Doyle, William (2001). The French Revolution: A very short introduction. Oxford University Press. ISBN 978-0-19-285396-7.

Doyle, William (2009). Aristocracy and its Enemies in the Age of Revolution. Oxford UP. ISBN 978-0-19-160971-8.

Dwyer, Philip (2008). Napoleon: The Path to Power 1769–1799. Yale University Press. ISBN 978-0-300-14820-6.

Ellis, Geoffrey (1997). Aston, Nigel (ed.). Religion according to Napoleon; the limitations of pragmatism in Religious Change in Europe 1650-1914: Essays for John McManners. Clarendon Press. ISBN 978-0198205968.

Fehér, Ferenc (1990). The French Revolution and the Birth of Modernity (1992 ed.). University of California Press. ISBN 978-0520071209.

Finley, Theresa; Franck, Raphael; Johnson, Noel (2017). "The Effects of Land Redistribution: Evidence from the French Revolution". George Mason University. SSRN 3033094.

Forster, Robert (1967). "The Survival of the Nobility during the French Revolution". Past & Present. 37 (37): 71–86. doi:10.1093/past/37.1.71. JSTOR 650023.

Franck, Raphaël; Michalopoulos, Stelios (2017). "Emigration during the French Revolution: Consequences in the Short and Longue Durée" (PDF). NBER Working Paper No. 23936. doi:10.3386/w23936. S2CID 134086399. Archived (PDF) from the original on 20 February 2018.

Fremont-Barnes, Gregory (2007). Encyclopedia of the Age of Political Revolutions and New Ideologies, 1760–1815. Greenwood. ISBN 978-0-313-04951-4.

Frey, Linda; Frey, Marsha (2004). The French Revolution. Greenwood Press. ISBN 978-0-313-32193-1.

Furet, François (1981). Interpreting the French Revolution. Cambridge UP.

Furet, François (1995). Revolutionary France, 1770–1880. Blackwell Publishing. ISBN 978-0-631-19808-6.

Furet, François (1989). Kafker, Frank (ed.). A Deep-rooted Ideology as Well as Circumstance in The French Revolution: Conflicting Interpretations (2002 ed.). Krieger Publishing Company. ISBN 978-1-57524-092-3.

Furet, François; Ozouf, Mona (1989). A Critical Dictionary of the French Revolution. Harvard University Press. ISBN 978-0-674-17728-4.

Fursenko, A.A; McArthur, Gilbert (1976). "The American and French Revolutions Compared: The View from the U.S.S.R." The William and Mary Quarterly. 33 (3): 481. doi:10.2307/1921544. JSTOR 1921544.

Garrioch, David (1994). "The People of Paris and Their Police in the Eighteenth Century. Reflections on the introduction of a 'modern' police force". European History Quarterly. 24 (4): 511–535. doi:10.1177/026569149402400402. S2CID 144460864.

Gershoy, Leo (1957). The Era of the French Revolution. New York: Van Nostrand. pp. 16–17, 23. ISBN 978-0898747188.

Goldhammer, Jesse (2005). The headless republic : sacrificial violence in modern French thought. Cornell University Press. ISBN 978-0-8014-4150-9. OCLC 783283094.

Gough, Hugh (1998). The Terror in the French Revolution (2010 ed.). Palgrave. ISBN 978-0-230-20181-1.

Greenwood, Frank Murray (1993). Legacies of Fear: Law and Politics in Quebec in the Era of the French Revolution. University of Toronto Press. ISBN 978-0-8020-6974-0.

Hampson, Norman (1988). A Social History of the French Revolution. Routledge: University of Toronto Press. ISBN 978-0-7100-6525-4.

Hanson, Paul (2009). Contesting the French Revolution. Blackwell Publishing. ISBN 978-1-4051-6083-4.

Hanson, Paul (2007). The A to Z of the French Revolution. Scarecrow Press. ISBN 978-1-4617-1606-8.

Harden, David J (1995). "Liberty Caps and Liberty Trees". Past & Present. 146 (146): 66–102. doi:10.1093/past/146.1.66. JSTOR 651152.

Hargreaves-Mawdsley, William (1968). Spain under the Bourbons, 1700–1833. Palgrave Macmillan.

Hayworth, Justin (2015). Conquering the natural frontier: French expansion to the Rhine during the War of the First Coalition 1792–1797 (PDF) (PHD). North Texas University. Archived (PDF) from the original on 24 March 2020.

Hibbert, Christopher (1980). The Days of the French Revolution. Quill, William Morrow. ISBN 978-0-688-03704-8.

Hibbert, Christopher (1982). The French Revolution. Penguin. ISBN 978-0-14-004945-9.

Horstboll, Henrik; Ostergård, Uffe (1990). "Reform and Revolution: The French Revolution and the Case of Denmark". Scandinavian Journal of History. 15 (3). doi:10.1080/03468759008579195.

Hufton, Olwen (1983). "Social Conflict and the Grain Supply in Eighteenth-Century France". The Journal of Interdisciplinary History. 14 (2): 303–331. doi:10.2307/203707. JSTOR 203707.

Hufton, Olwen (1992). Women and the Limits of Citizenship in the French Revolution. University of Toronto Press. ISBN 978-0-8020-6837-8.

Hunt, Lynn (1996). The French Revolution and Human Rights (2016 ed.). Bedford/St Martins. ISBN 978-1-319-04903-4.

Hunt, Lynn (1984). Politics, Culture, and Class in the French Revolution. University of California Press.

Hunt, Lynn; Lansky, David; Hanson, Paul (1979). "The Failure of the Liberal Republic in France, 1795–1799: The Road to Brumaire". The Journal of Modern History. 51 (4): 734–759. doi:10.1086/241988. JSTOR 1877164. S2CID 154019725.

Hunt, Lynn; Martin, Thomas R; Rosenwein, Barbara H. (2003). The Making of the West; Volume II (2010 ed.). Bedford Press. ISBN 978-0-312-55460-6.

Hussenet, Jacques (2007). "Détruisez la Vendée !" Regards croisés sur les victimes et destructions de la guerre de Vendée (in French). Centre vendéen de recherches historiques.

James, C. L. R. (1963). The Black Jacobins: Toussaint L'Ouverture and the San Domingo Revolution (2001 ed.). Penguin Books.

Jefferson, Thomas (1903). Ford, Paul (ed.). The Works of Thomas Jefferson, Vol. XII: Correspondence and Papers 1808–1816 (2010 ed.). Cosimo Classics. ISBN 978-1-61640-215-0.

Jones, Peter M (1988). The Peasantry in the French Revolution. Cambridge UP. ISBN 978-0-521-33070-1.

Jordan, David (2004). The King's Trial: The French Revolution versus Louis XVI. University of California Press. ISBN 978-0-520-23697-4.

Jourdan, Annie (2007). "The "Alien Origins" of the French Revolution: American, Scottish, Genevan, and Dutch Influences". The Western Society for French History. University of Amsterdam. 35 (2). hdl:2027/spo.0642292.0035.012.

Kennedy, Emmet (1989). A Cultural History of the French Revolution. Yale University Press. ISBN 978-0-300-04426-3.

Kennedy, Michael (2000). The Jacobin Clubs in the French Revolution: 1793–1795. Berghahn Books. ISBN 978-1-57181-186-8.

Keitner, Chimene I (2007). The Paradoxes of Nationalism: The French Revolution and Its Meaning for Contemporary Nation Building. SUNY Press. ISBN 978-0-7914-6958-3.

Kołakowski, Leszek (1978). Main Currents of Marxism: The Founders, the Golden Age, the Breakdown. W.W. Norton. ISBN 978-0-393-06054-6.

Kossmann, E.H. (1978). The Low Countries: 1780–1940. Clarendon Press. ISBN 978-0-19-822108-1.

Lalevée, Thomas J (2019). National Pride and Republican grandezza: Brissot's New Language for International Politics in the French Revolution (PDF) (PHD). Australian National University.

Lefebvre, Georges (1962). The French Revolution: From Its Origins to 1793. Columbia University Press. ISBN 978-0-231-08598-4.

Lefebvre, Georges (1963). The French Revolution: from 1793 to 1799. Vol. II. New York: Columbia University Press. ISBN 978-0-231-02519-5.

Lefebvre, Georges (1964). The Thermidorians & the Directory. Random House. ISBN 9780134445397.

Lefebvre, Georges (1947). The Coming of the French Revolution (2005 ed.). Princeton UP. ISBN 978-0-691-12188-8.

Léonard, Jacques (1977). "Femmes, Religion et Médecine: Les Religieuses qui Soignent, en France au XIXe Siècle". Annales: Économies, Sociétés, Civilisations (in French). 32 (55).

Levy, Darline Gay; Applewhite, Harriet Branson; Johnson, Mary Durham, eds. (1979). Women in Revolutionary Paris, 1789–1795. University of Illinois Press. ISBN 978-0252004094.

Lewis, Gwynne (2002). The French Revolution: Rethinking the Debate. Routledge. ISBN 978-0-203-40991-6.

Livesey, James (2001). Making Democracy in the French Revolution. Harvard University Press. ISBN 978-0-674-00624-9.

Ludwikowski, Rhett (1990). "The French Declaration of the Rights of Man and Citizen and the American Constitutional Development". The American Journal of Comparative Law. 2: 445–

462. doi:10.2307/840552. JSTOR 840552. S2CID 143656851.

Lyons, Martyn (1975). France under the Directory (2008 ed.). Cambridge University Press. ISBN 978-0-521-09950-9.

Martin, Jean-Clément (1987). La Vendée et la France (in French). Éditions du Seuil.

Marx, Karl (1983). Kamenka, Eugene (ed.). The Paris Commune and the Future of Socialism: 1870–1882 in The Portable Karl Marx. Penguin Books. ISBN 978-0140150964.

McHugh, Tim (2012). "Expanding Women's Rural Medical Work in Early Modern Brittany: The Daughters of the Holy Spirit". History of Medicine and Allied Sciences. 67 (3): 428–456. doi:10.1093/jhmas/jrr032. PMC 3376001. PMID 21724643.

McLynn, Frank (1997). Napoleon (1998 ed.). Pimlico. ISBN 978-0-7126-6247-5.

McManners, John (1969). The French Revolution and the Church (1982 ed.). Praeger. ISBN 978-0-313-23074-5.

McMillan, James H (1999). France and women, 1789–1914: gender, society and politics. Routledge. ISBN 978-0-415-22602-8.

Melzer, Sarah; Rabine, Leslie, eds. (1992). Rebel Daughters: Women and the French Revolution. Oxford University Press Inc. ISBN 978-0-19-506886-3.

McPhee, Peter, ed. (2012). A Companion to the French Revolution. Wiley-Blackwell. ISBN 978-1-4443-3564-4.

Mitchell, CJ (1984). "Political Divisions within the Legislative Assembly of 1791". French Historical Studies. 13 (3): 356–389. doi:10.2307/286298. JSTOR 286298.

Neely, Sylvia (2008). A Concise History of the French Revolution. Rowman & Littlefield. ISBN 978-0-7425-3411-7.

Palmer, RR (1986). "How Five Centuries of Educational Philanthropy Disappeared in the French Revolution". History of Education Quarterly. 26 (2): 181–197. doi:10.2307/368736. JSTOR 368736. S2CID 147116875.

Palmer, Robert; Colton, Joel (1995). A History of the Modern World. Alfred A Knopf. ISBN 978-0-679-43253-1.

Pelling, Nick (2002). Anglo-Irish Relations: 1798-1922. Routledge. ISBN 978-0203986554.

Price, Munro (2003). The Road from Versailles: Louis XVI, Marie Antoinette, and the Fall of the French Monarchy. St Martins Press. ISBN 978-0-312-26879-4.

Riemer, Neal; Simon, Douglas (1997). The New World of Politics: An Introduction to Political Science. Rowman & Littlefield. ISBN 978-0-939693-41-2.

Rossignol, Marie-Jeanne (2006). The American Revolution in France: Under the Shadow of the French Revolution in Europe's American Revolution. ISBN 978-0-230-28845-4.

Rothenberg, Gunter (1988). "The Origins, Causes, and Extension of the Wars of the French Revolution and Napoleon". The Journal of Interdisciplinary History. 18 (4): 771–793. doi:10.2307/204824. JSTOR 204824.

Rude, George (1991). The French Revolution: Its Causes, Its History and Its Legacy After 200 Years. Grove Press. ISBN 978-0-8021-3272-7.

Sargent, Thomas J; Velde, Francois R (1995). "Macroeconomic features of the French Revolution". Journal of Political Economy. 103 (3): 474–518. doi:10.1086/261992. S2CID 153904650.

Schama, Simon (1989). Citizens, A Chronicle of The French Revolution (2004 ed.). Penguin. ISBN 978-0-14-101727-3.

Schama, Simon (1977). Patriots and Liberators: Revolution in the Netherlands, 1780–1813. Harper Collins. ISBN 978-0-00-216701-7.

Shlapentokh, Dmitry (1996). "A problem in self-identity: Russian intellectual thought in the context of the French Revolution". European Studies. 26 (1): 061–76. doi:10.1177/004724419602600104. S2CID 145177231.

Scott, Samuel (1975). "Problems of Law and Order during 1790, the "Peaceful" Year of the French Revolution". The American Historical Review. 80 (4): 859–888. doi:10.2307/1867442. JSTOR 1867442.

Shusterman, Noah (2013). The French Revolution; Faith, Desire, and Politics. Routledge. ISBN 978-0-415-66021-1.

Soboul, Albert (1975). The French Revolution 1787–1799. Vintage. ISBN 978-0-394-71220-8.

Soboul, Albert (1977). A short history of the French Revolution: 1789–1799. Geoffrey Symcox. University of California Press, Ltd. ISBN 978-0-520-03419-8.

Soper, J. Christopher; Fetzer, Joel S (2003). "Explaining the accommodation of Muslim religious practices in France, Britain, and Germany". French Politics. 1 (1): 39–59. doi:10.1057/palgrave.fp.8200018. S2CID 145008815.

Spang, Rebecca (2003). "Paradigms and Paranoia: How modern Is the French Revolution?". American Historical Review. 108 (1). doi:10.1086/ahr/108.1.119.

Stewart, John (1951). A Documentary Survey of the French revolution. Macmillan.

Sutherland, D. M. G. (2002). "Peasants, Lords, and Leviathan: Winners and Losers from the Abolition of French Feudalism, 1780–1820". The Journal of Economic History. 62 (1): 1–24. JSTOR 2697970.

Tackett, Timothy (2003). "The Flight to Varennes and the Coming of the Terror". Historical Reflections / Réflexions Historiques. 29 (3): 469–493. JSTOR 41299285.

Tackett, Timothy (2004). When the King Took Flight. Harvard University Press. ISBN 978-0-674-01642-2.

Tackett, Timothy (2011). "Rumor and Revolution: The Case of the September Massacres" (PDF). French History and Civilization. 4. Archived (PDF) from the original on 30 November 2018.

Thompson, J.M. (1959). The French Revolution. Basil Blackwell.

Thompson, J.M. (1952). Robespierre and the French Revolution. The English Universities Press. ISBN 978-0340083697.

Tilly, Louise (1983). "Food Entitlement, Famine, and Conflict". The Journal of Interdisciplinary History. 14 (2): 333–349. doi:10.2307/203708. JSTOR 203708.

Tombs, Robert; Tombs, Isabelle (2007). That Sweet Enemy: The French and the British from the Sun King to the Present. Random House. ISBN 978-1-4000-4024-7.

Vardi, Liana (1988). "The Abolition of the Guilds during the French Revolution". French Historical Studies. 15 (4): 704–717. doi:10.2307/286554. JSTOR 286554.

Wasson, Ellis (2009). A History of Modern Britain: 1714 to the Present. John Wiley & Sons. ISBN 978-1-4051-3935-9.

Weir, David (1989). "Tontines, Public Finance, and Revolution in France and England, 1688–1789". The Journal of Economic History. 49 (1): 95–124. doi:10.1017/S002205070000735X. JSTOR 2121419. S2CID 154494955.

White, Eugene Nelson (1995). "The French Revolution and the Politics of Government Finance, 1770–1815". The Journal of Economic History. 55 (2): 227–255. doi:10.1017/S0022050700041048. JSTOR 2123552. S2CID 154871390.

Woronoff, Denis (1984). The Thermidorean regime and the directory: 1794–1799. Cambridge University Press. ISBN 978-0-521-28917-7.

Printed in Great Britain
by Amazon

38777746R00079